MW00896674

LLM Prompt Engineering For Developers

The Art and Science of Unlocking LLMs' True Potential

Aymen El Amri @eon01

LLM Prompt Engineering For Developers

The Art and Science of Unlocking LLMs' True Potential

Aymen El Amri @eon01

ISBN 9798859940714

Published by FAUN: Pioneering the future of developer growth. At FAUN, we empower developers by keeping them at the forefront of what truly matters in the ever-evolving tech landscape.

Contents

1: Preface

Many of you may have probably experimented with ChatGPT or other Large Language Models (LLMs) and initially been swept up in the excitement. The initial "wow" effect was undeniable. Yet, after a few interactions, the shine began to wear off. You might have noticed its quirks and inconsistencies, realizing that, in its raw form, it doesn't seamlessly fit into our daily tasks.

text-davinci-003 fail

Have you ever asked a language model to write a blog post on a specific topic, only to receive a response that was off-mark or lacked depth? Or perhaps you asked it to summarize a long and complex article, and instead of a concise summary, you got a jumbled mix of sentences lacking the main points. Such experiences can be frustrating, especially when you know the potential that lies within these models.

You may have searched for "perfect" prompts in online prompt database - a new phenomenon that has emerged in the wake of ChatGPT's and other LLMs' popularity - hoping for a quick solution. However, you soon realize that what works for one person may not work for another.

Each prompt is unique and tailored to specific needs and contexts. It is a mistake to assume that the one-size-fits-all approach will always work. In all cases, be assured: This guide goes beyond just providing prompts and is not a collection of prompts. Instead, it explains the "how" behind crafting effective prompts. With this knowledge and skill, you can create prompts that align with your objectives and lead to better interactions with LLMs.

In reality, if you were sometimes disappointed, it's not entirely the LLM's fault. The key lies in how we communicate with it. Just as we need to frame our questions correctly when seeking answers from a search engine, we need to craft our prompts effectively for ChatGPT or any other LLM for that matter. It's just that search engines do not need as much guidance as LLMs do. This art of guiding LLMs and optimizing our interactions with them is more than just a technique; it's a paradigm shift, a new experimental science that we call "Prompt Engineering".

In fact, it emphasizes the importance of clear, structured communication with AI. As developers, we're not just coding; we're teaching, guiding, and refining the AI's understanding. This guide, "LLM Prompt Engineering For Developers", is your comprehensive guide to mastering this emerging discipline. Dive in, and discover how to unlock the true potential of ChatGPT and similar models, making them invaluable tools in your development arsenal.

The art of communicating with LLMs relies heavily on prompt engineering. Consider it like finding the perfect key for a lock. While humans can interpret vague or incomplete information, LLMs require precise instructions to deliver optimal results. The goal isn't to converse in human terms but to effectively translate our needs into a language the model understands.

Often, individuals approach LLMs as if they're interacting with another human, projecting their own thought processes and expecting similar interpretations. However, this anthropomorphic perspective can be misleading. Instead of expecting the LLM to think like us, we must strive to understand its "logic" so that it can better serve our needs. This mutual understanding is the essence of prompt engineering. By refining our prompts, we guide the LLM to produce the most relevant and insightful responses.

Prompt engineering is not an isolated discipline; it stands at the intersection of several fields, each contributing unique insights. From Artificial Intelligence algorithms to data-driven strategies in Data Science and predictive models in

Machine Learning, prompt engineering draws from a rich tapestry of knowledge. This multidisciplinary nature might seem daunting at first, suggesting a steep learning curve that requires expertise in various domains.

To excel in this field, it is essential to possess robust skills in Artificial Intelligence, Data Science, and Machine Learning. Proficiency in these areas is invaluable for comprehending the workings of generative AIs and writing prompts with greater precision and accuracy.

However, this guide, "LLM Prompt Engineering For Developers," aims to demystify the complexity of prompt engineering. Its goal is to distill the essence of prompt engineering into its most accessible form. While a foundational understanding of these disciplines certainly aids in mastering prompt engineering, it's not a strict prerequisite to start practicing and seeing tangible results.

"LLM Prompt Engineering For Developers" is designed to be a bridge, allowing anyone with a basic grasp of programming to dive into the world of prompt engineering and prompt engineering agility. Through clear explanations, practical examples, and step-by-step hands-on labs, we'll simplify the journey, ensuring that you not only understand the core concepts but also feel empowered to take your first steps in this exciting field.

1.1: What are you going to learn?

In "LLM Prompt Engineering For Developers," we take a comprehensive journey into the world of LLMs and the art of crafting effective prompts for them.

The guide starts by laying the foundation, exploring the evolution of Natural Language Processing (NLP) from its early days to the sophisticated LLMs we interact with today. You will dive deep into the complexities of models such as GPT models, understanding their architecture, capabilities, and nuances.

As we progress, this guide emphasizes the importance of effective prompt engineering and its best practices. While LLMs like ChatGPT (gpt-3.5) are powerful, their full potential is only realized when they are communicated with effectively. This is where prompt engineering comes into play. It's not simply about asking the model a question; it's about phrasing, context, and understanding the model's logic.

Through chapters dedicated to Azure Prompt Flow, LangChain, and other tools, you'll gain hands-on experience in crafting, testing, scoring and optimizing prompts. We'll also explore advanced concepts like Few-shot Learning, Chain of Thought, Perplexity and techniques like ReAct and General Knowledge Prompting, equipping you with a comprehensive understanding of the domain.

This guide is designed to be hands-on, offering practical insights and exercises. In fact, as you progress, you'll familiarize yourself with several tools:

- **openai Python library**: You will dive into the core of OpenAI's LLMs and learn how to interact and fine-tune models to achieve precise outputs tailored to specific needs.
- **promptfoo**: You will master the art of crafting effective prompts. Throughout the guide, we'll use promptfoo to test and score prompts, ensuring they're optimized for desired outcomes.
- **LangChain**: You'll explore the LangChain framework, which elevates LLM-powered applications. You'll dive into understanding how a prompt engineer can leverage the power of this tool to test and build effective prompts.
- **betterprompt**: Before deploying, it's essential to test. With betterprompt, you'll ensure the LLM prompts are ready for real-world scenarios, refining them as needed.
- **Azure Prompt Flow**: You will experience the visual interface of Azure's tool, streamlining LLM-based AI development. You'll design executable flows, integrating LLMs, prompts, and Python tools, ensuring a holistic understanding of the art of prompting.
- And more!

With these tools in your toolkit, you will be well-prepared to craft powerful and effective prompts. The hands-on exercises will help solidify your understanding. Throughout the process, you'll be actively engaged and by the end, not only will you appreciate the power of prompt engineering, but you'll also possess the skills to implement it effectively.

1.2: To whom is this guide for?

This guide is designed for those passionate about LLMs and the emerging field of prompt engineering. Regardless of your AI expertise or familiarity with programming, this guide provides a clear route to mastering the nuances of creating effective prompts for LLMs. So if you are a beginner, don't worry. We'll start from the basics and build up from there. For those eager to unlock the vast capabilities of language models in practical scenarios, consider this guide your essential starting point.

1.3: Join the community

This guide was published by FAUN, a community of developers, architects, and software engineers who are passionate about learning and sharing their knowledge. If you are interested in joining the community, you can start by subscribing to our newsletter at faun.dev/join[1]. Every week, we share the most important and relevant articles, tutorials, and videos on the latest technologies and trends including AI, ML, and NLP. You can also follow us on Twitter at @faun_dev[2] and LinkedIn[3] to stay up to date with the latest news and announcements.

1.4: About the author

Aymen El Amri is a polymath software engineer, author, and entrepreneur. He is the founder of FAUN Developer Community. He is also the author of multiple books on software engineering. You can find him on Twitter[4] and LinkedIn[5].

---

[1] https://faun.dev/join
[2] https://twitter.com/joinFAUN
[3] https://www.linkedin.com/company/22322295
[4] https://twitter.com/eon01
[5] https://www.linkedin.com/in/elamriaymen/

2: From NLP to Large Language Models

2.1: What is Natural Language Processing?

Natural language refers to the language used by humans to communicate with each other. It encompasses spoken and written language, as well as sign language. The natural language is distinct from formal language, which is used in mathematics and computer programming.

Generative AI systems, specifically ChatGPT, are capable of understanding and producing natural language as well as formal language. In both cases, interactive AI assistants like ChatGPT use the natural language to communicate with humans. Their output could be a natural language response or a mix between natural and formal languages.

To process, understand and generate natural language, a whole field of AI has emerged: Natural Language Processing (NLP). NLP, by definition, is the field of artificial intelligence that focuses on the understanding and generation of human language by computers. It is employed in a wide range of applications, including voice assistants, machine translation, chatbots, and more. In other words, when we talk about NLP, we refer to computers' ability to understand and generate natural language.

NLP has experienced rapid growth in recent years, largely due to advancements in language models such as GPT and BERT. These models are some of the most powerful NLP models to date. But what is a language model?

2.2: Language models

Models are intelligent computer programs that can perform a specific task. For example, a model can be trained to recognize images of cats and dogs, to write social media posts or blog posts, to provide medical assistance or legal advice, and so on.

These models are the result of a training process that uses large datasets to teach the model how to perform a specific task. The larger the dataset, the more accurate the model will be. This is why models trained on large datasets are often more accurate than models trained on smaller datasets.

Using the dataset used for training, models acquire the capability of performing predictions on new data. For example, a model trained on a dataset of images of cats and dogs can predict whether a new image contains a cat or a dog.

Language models are a subset of models that are capable of generating, understanding, or manipulating text or speech in natural language. These models are essential in the field of NLP and are used in various applications such as machine translation, speech recognition, text generation, chatbots, and more.

Here are some types of language models:

- Statistical models (n-grams)
- Neural network-based models

  - Feedforward neural networks
  - Recurrent neural networks (RNNs)
  - Long short-term memory (LSTM)
  - Gated recurrent units (GRUs)

- Knowledge-based models
- Contextual language models
- Transformer models

  - Bidirectional encoder representations from transformers (BERT)
  - Generative pre-trained transformer (GPT)

2.3: Statistical models (n-grams)

Statistical models like n-gram models serve as foundational language models commonly used for text classification and language modeling. They can also be adapted for text generation, although more advanced models are typically better suited for complex text-to-text tasks. Within statistical models, word sequence probabilities are derived from training data, enabling the model to estimate the likelihood of the next word in a sequence.

N-gram models specifically consider the preceding n-1 words when estimating the probability of the next word. For instance, a bigram model takes into account only the preceding single word, while a trigram model examines the two preceding words. This characteristic endows n-gram models with quick training and utilization capabilities, but they exhibit limitations in capturing long-range dependencies.

In a trigram model, each current word is paired with the two preceding words, forming sequences of three words. For instance, in the sentence "A man of knowledge restrains his words," the observed trigrams would include "A man of," "man of knowledge," "of knowledge restrains," "knowledge restrains his," and "restrains his words." These sequential 3-word patterns are then employed by the model to estimate the probabilities of subsequent words.

Rather than clustering words, n-gram models leverage local word order and context derived from the training data. By focusing on these short-term sequences, n-gram models can make predictions about forthcoming words without modeling global semantics. Although they are efficient and straightforward, their local context renders them less suitable for generating lengthy texts.

Statistical models, particularly n-grams, are quite different from the more recent neural language models, and the concept of "prompt engineering" as it's understood today is more closely associated with the latter. However, there are ways in which the design of input or the preprocessing of data for n-gram models can be thought of as a precursor to prompt engineering.

2.4: Knowledge-based models

These models combine NLP techniques with a structured knowledge base, enabling them to perform tasks that require deeper understanding and reasoning. They are more useful in specific domains such as medicine or law.

2.5: Contextual language models

These models can understand the meaning of words based on their context. ELMo[6] (Embeddings from Language MOdels) is an example of a contextual language model. ELMo is primarily used to obtain word representations that take context into account. These representations can then be used in various NLP tasks such as text classification, named entity recognition, and more.

2.6: Neural network-based models

Neural network-based models are models that learn and process information in a way inspired by the human brain. They are designed to recognize patterns and make predictions based on large amounts of data. These models consist of interconnected artificial neurons that work together to solve tasks such as image recognition, natural language processing, voice recognition and more!

Neural network-based models are used in various applications, including self-driving cars, virtual assistants, and recommendation systems. They enable computers to learn from examples and improve their performance over time.

2.6.1: Feedforward neural networks

Feedforward neural networks are the simplest type of neural network. They consist of an input layer, one or more hidden layers, and an output layer. The input layer receives the input data, which is then passed through the hidden layers to the output layer.

---

[6]https://en.wikipedia.org/wiki/ELMo

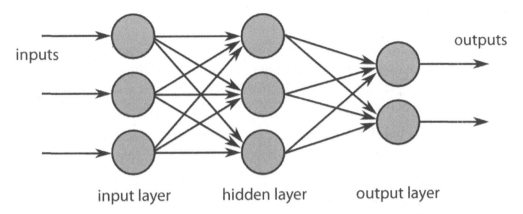

inputs

outputs

input layer   hidden layer   output layer

Multilayer Neural Network

Each layer consists of a set of neurons that perform a specific task. The neurons in the input layer receive the input data and pass it to the neurons in the hidden layers. The neurons in the hidden layers perform calculations on the input data and pass the results to the neurons in the output layer. The neurons in the output layer perform calculations on the results and produce the final output.

This type of neural network can be used for tasks such as image recognition, speech recognition, and other simple classification tasks however, it is not suitable for more complex tasks.

2.6.2: Recurrent neural networks (RNNs)

Recurrent Neural Networks (RNNs) were created to overcome the limitations of traditional feedforward neural networks in handling sequential data. Unlike feedforward networks, which process inputs independently, RNNs have the ability to retain information from previous steps in the sequence. This is what makes them well-suited for handling sequential data like text and speech.

They are used in various applications such as translation, sentiment analysis and text to speech processing.

 Sequential data is data that is ordered in a particular way and each element in the sequence has a specific meaning. For example, a sentence is a sequence of words and each word has a specific meaning.

2.6.3: Long short-term memory (LSTM)

Long Short-Term Memory (LSTM) is a special type of neural network that is good at understanding and remembering information in sequences of data. It was created to solve a problem that regular neural networks have with remembering things over long periods.

Regular neural networks can sometimes forget important information when dealing with sequences. But LSTM is designed to remember important details and pass them along through many steps in the sequence.

This makes LSTM useful for tasks where understanding the order and context of the data is important, like language translation, speech recognition, and predicting the next word in a sentence.

[i] LSTM is like a smart memory that helps the neural network remember things in the right order and context.

They can be used in text generation tasks. While you can provide an LSTM with an initial sequence (akin to a "prompt") to generate or classify subsequent sequences, the nuanced manipulation of this initial sequence to guide the LSTM's output isn't typically referred to as "prompt engineering."

2.6.4: Gated recurrent units (GRUs)

Gated Recurrent Units (GRUs) are a type of neural network architecture designed to process sequences of data, much like Long Short-Term Memory (LSTM) networks. One of the primary motivations behind the development of GRUs was to address some of the complexities and computational demands of LSTMs, while still effectively capturing long-term dependencies in sequential data. As a result, GRUs have a more streamlined structure than LSTMs, which often allows them to train faster and require fewer computational resources. A key feature of GRUs is the use of "gates."

[i] Think of gates as checkpoints that regulate the flow of information within the network. They determine what data should be retained, updated, or discarded as the sequence is processed. This mechanism ensures that the network focuses on relevant details and can recall important information from earlier in the sequence.

GRUs have proven valuable in a variety of tasks that require understanding sequences, such as language processing, speech recognition, and more. Their ability to recognize patterns and relationships in sequential data makes them a popular choice for many applications in the realm of deep learning.

Text generation is one such application but the manipulation of the initial sequence to guide the GRU's output isn't typically referred to as "prompt engineering."

2.7: Transformer models

Imagine you're reading a book, word by word. You understand each word, but you don't understand the meaning of the whole sentence. You need to read the whole sentence to understand it. Similarly, you need to read the whole paragraph to understand the meaning of the whole paragraph. And you need to read the whole book to understand the meaning of the whole book. This is naturally, how humans read and understand a book. The basic idea here is that you need to read the whole text to understand it and it all starts with understanding each word and how it relates to the other words around it.

The transformer acts in a similar way. Instead of reading word by word, it can look at many words at once and understand how they relate to each other. This is called "attention".

A few years ago, some researchers at Google came up with a new way to read text. They called it the "transformer" and it was explained in a paper called 'Attention Is All You Need[7]' by Ashish Vaswani et al., Google Brain team.

Before this, there were other ways to read and understand text, like something called LSTM. But this new transformer idea was faster and better!

Here's an example: Imagine the sentence "The cat sat on the ___." Even if you hide the last word, you can guess it might be "mat" because of the words before it. The transformer does this by looking at all the words, understanding their relationship, and making a smart guess.

Now, this transformer idea became super popular. People started using it not just for reading text, but also for computer visions, biological sequence analysis and more.

---

[7]https://arxiv.org/pdf/1706.03762.pdf

Because of how effective transformers are, companies started building big models using them, we call these models "Large Language Models". Two famous ones are BERT and GPT.

2.7.1: Bidirectional encoder representations from transformers (BERT)

BERT[8] is an advanced language model that understands words based on their entire context, considering both preceding and following words in a sentence. This bidirectional understanding allows BERT to grasp the specific meaning of words based on their surroundings.

Developed using a neural network architecture called the Transformer, BERT has been trained on vast amounts of text. During its training, some words in the text are intentionally hidden, and BERT tries to predict them based on their context, helping it learn word relationships and meanings.

Created by researchers at Google, BERT can be fine-tuned for various tasks. It's commonly adapted for sentiment analysis, question answering, and identifying named entities like people, places, or organizations in text.

Even if it's possible to fine-tune it to be a language model, BERT is not typically used for text generation tasks mainly because of its bidirectional nature. Traditional LMs typically generate text in a unidirectional manner, predicting the next word based on previous words. BERT's bidirectional nature makes it great for tasks like understanding and classifying existing text but less suited for generating coherent and fluent sequences of new text.

BERT is a high-capacity model designed to **understand** sophisticated text.

2.7.2: Generative pre-trained transformer (GPT)

GPT is a language model that can generate text based on a given prompt. It is trained on a large amount of text and can generate text that is similar to the text it was trained on.

---

[8]https://github.com/google-research/bert

GPT-3 and GPT-4 are the latest versions of GPT. They are powerful language models with a lot of parameters. They are built on the same architecture as GPT-2[9] but with some changes. GPT-3 and GPT-4 use a mix of dense and sparse attention patterns in their layers, which helps the model process information efficiently.

Unlike BERT, GPT is a high-capacity model designed to **generate** sophisticated text.

Prompt engineering is highly relevant to GPT-based models, as it can be used to guide the model's output and produce more relevant and coherent text. When we talk about prompt engineering, we are typically referring to the manipulation of the initial sequence to guide the GPT's output. This involves carefully crafting the input to elicit a specific type of response or to steer the model's behavior in a desired direction. The better the prompt, the more accurate and contextually relevant the output from GPT tends to be.

As GPT models, especially GPT-3 and GPT-4, have grown in size and capability, the importance of effective prompt engineering has also increased. This is because these models have a vast amount of knowledge and potential responses, so guiding them effectively can be the difference between a generic answer and a highly specific, relevant one. Moreover, with the right prompts, GPT models can perform tasks beyond mere text generation, such as answering questions, providing summaries, translating languages, and even some forms of reasoning.

2.8: What's next?

In this section, we learned about the different types of language models and how they are used in various applications. We also learned about that prompt engineering tightly relates to generative models, as it can be used to guide the model's output and produce more relevant and coherent text.

In the next section, we will learn more about prompt engineering.

---

[9]https://github.com/openai/gpt-2

3: Introduction to prompt engineering

Prompt engineering is an emerging discipline in the field of artificial intelligence. Its focus is on creating and optimizing instructions given to a language model, such as ChatGPT. Relevant and well-formulated prompts can influence the responses generated by the model, thus improving the quality and relevance of the results.

To be effective, prompt engineering requires an understanding of the underlying model, as well as an analysis of the training data to identify potential biases. By adjusting the instructions and model parameters, prompt engineers can shape the behavior of AI to more accurately meet user needs and produce more consistent and reliable results.

In a tweet, Sam Altman, CEO of OpenAI, described prompt engineering as "amazingly high-leverage skill and an early example of programming in a little bit of natural language."

Prompt Engineering according to Sam Altman

Prompt engineering is a critical discipline that has gained significant attention in recent years. As AI language models, such as GPT-4 and ChatGPT, have become more powerful and widely used, the importance of effectively guiding these models with carefully crafted instructions, known as prompts, has grown exponentially.

Language models are trained on vast amounts of text data to learn patterns, language structures, and context. However, generating coherent and contextually relevant responses from these models can be a complex task, as they may produce outputs that are either irrelevant or biased, especially when given ambiguous or poorly formulated prompts.

The history of prompt engineering can be traced back to the early stages of language model development. As AI researchers and developers sought to make language models more useful and user-friendly, they recognized the need for influencing the generated text by providing explicit instructions or context. Initially, simple prompts were used to guide the models, but they often led to generic or inadequate responses.

GPT-4, LaMDA, Llama 2 and PaLM language models were the most important milestones in the emergence of this field. These models were trained on large amounts of text data and were able to generate coherent and contextually relevant responses. Speculations suggest that GPT-4 boasts an astounding 170 trillion parameters. In comparison, Llama's most expansive version encompasses 65 billion parameters, while PaLM, a 540 billion parameter transformer model from Google, drives its AI chatbot, Bard, with exceptional genius. However, these models still required explicit instructions to produce desired outputs, this is what led to the development of prompt engineering as a new discipline.

This field has even more relevance after the release of text-to-image models like Stable Diffusion, Midjourney, and DALL-E. These models can generate images from text prompts, but they require specific instructions to produce desired outputs.

Over time, prompt engineering has evolved significantly, borrowing insights from various other related fields, such as NLP, computational linguistics, and human-computer interaction. Researchers have explored different strategies to design prompts that elicit precise and contextually accurate responses.

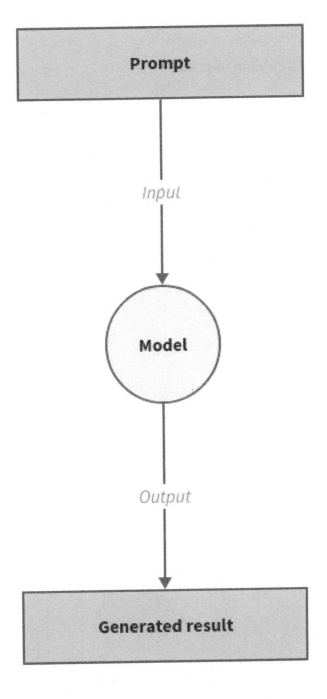

There are many challenges associated with prompt engineering - we are going to discover them in the next sections but the main point here is the lack of a unique standardized approach to prompt engineering. There are no clear guidelines or best practices for designing prompts, which makes it difficult to compare results across different models and applications.

To address these challenges, different prompt engineering techniques have matured to incorporate a diverse range of approaches.

This is what we will cover in this guide.

4: OpenAI GPT and Prompting: An Introduction

4.1: Generative Pre-trained Transformers (GPT) models

Generative Pre-trained Transformers models like GPT-4 are an important advancement in AI developed by OpenAI company. As part of the GPT (Generative Pre-trained Transformer) model family, ChatGPT (gpt-3.5) is specifically designed for generating text in a conversational manner.

With a vast dataset and sophisticated training, ChatGPT can understand user queries and provide relevant and often detailed responses.

From assisting with specific tasks to providing information on a variety of subjects, ChatGPT finds applications in various domains such as customer support, education, SEO, content creation, and much more. Its capabilities position it as a central element in the evolution of human-machine interactions.

4.2: What is GPT and how it is different from ChatGPT?

GPT stands for Generative Pre-trained Transformer. This architecture (transformer) is specifically designed for processing and generating natural language, making it proficient in understanding and producing human-like text.

The three terms in "Generative Pre-trained Transformer" have specific meanings:

- **Generative**: This means that GPT is capable of generating text **autonomously**. It can produce new sentences, paragraphs, or even articles **that did not exist before** based on the data it has been trained on.

- **Pre-trained**: Before being used for specific tasks, GPT is pre-trained on a **very large dataset of textual data**. This enables it to learn patterns, structures, and general information about language.
- **Transformer**: This is the type of neural network architecture used by this type of models. Transformer architectures are particularly effective in processing sequences of data, such as text, and are known for their ability to capture long-term dependencies in the data.

GPT has evolved through different versions, with GPT-2 and GPT-3 being among the most well-known prior to the arrival of GPT-4. Each successive version of GPT tends to be larger in terms of parameter count and trained on more data, generally resulting in improved performance on various natural language processing tasks.

While GPT-2, GPT-3 and GPT-4 are language models, ChatGPT is web application that uses GPT-3.5-turbo to generate text in a conversational manner. GPT-3.5 is a set of models that improve on GPT-3 and can understand as well as generate natural language or code. With the release of gpt-3.5-turbo, OpenAI is gradually depreciating GPT-3 in favor of GPT-3.5 and GPT-4.

4.3: The GPT models series: a closer look

After understanding the difference between GPT-x models and ChatGPT, it is time to take a closer look at the GPT model family. This will help you understand the ecosystem of GPT models and how they are related to each other.

Traditionally, when a new model is released after a process involving research, training and development, it is deployed in an infrastructure (such as a cloud service) and made available to developers and users. To use the model, a developer needs to integrate it into their application or service. There are many ways to do this, but the most common approach is to use an API (Application Programming Interface).

An API is a set of functions and procedures that allow developers to access the functionality of a system. In the case of GPT models, the API is used to send text to the model and receive the generated text in response. This is how developers can integrate GPT models into their applications and services.

The OpenAI API is powered by a diverse set of models with different capabilities and price ranges. You can also make limited customizations to the original base models for your specific use case through a process called fine-tuning.

Fine-tuning is a process that involves training a model on a specific dataset to adapt it to a particular task. For example, you can fine-tune a GPT model on a dataset of movie reviews to create a movie review generator. This is a common practice in the field of Natural Language Processing. However, it requires programming skills.

In the following sections, we will take a closer look at the different models in the GPT family. Even if you are not a developer, this will help you understand the capabilities of each model and how they can be used in different applications. The knowledge you gain here will also help you make better decisions when choosing a GPT model for your project.

4.3.1: GPT-3.5

GPT-3.5 models can understand and generate both natural language and code. They are optimized for conversations but are also effective for traditional text completion tasks.

Among the base models of GPT-3.5 is the gpt-3.5-turbo model.

gpt-3.5-turbo is the highest-performing model in the GPT-3.5 range, optimized for chat, and costs one-tenth the price of text-davinci-003.

> text-davinci-003 is a model in the GPT-3 family that is optimized for text completion and generation tasks. It used to be the most powerful model in all GPT-3 models, but it is also one of the most expensive. However, as said, it is now being depreciated and is considered as a legacy model.

According to OpenAI, gpt-3.5-turbo is now one of the most powerful and cost-effective model in the GPT-3.5 family.

4.3.2: GPT-4

GPT-4 is a large multimodal model (accepting textual inputs and producing textual outputs currently, with support for image inputs coming in the future) that can solve difficult problems with greater precision than any previous models, thanks to its broader general knowledge and advanced reasoning capabilities.

Like gpt-3.5-turbo, GPT-4 is optimized for chat but also performs well on traditional text completion tasks. It can also solve problems in logic, mathematics, science, and even generate computer programs.

4.3.3: Other models

- GPT-3: A set of models capable of understanding and generating natural language. Some examples of models in this series are text-davinci-003, text-davinci-002, code-davinci-002, text-curie-001, text-babbage-001 and text-ada-001.
- DALL-E: An image generation model that can create images from textual descriptions. It can generate high-quality images in a wide variety of styles, sizes, and resolutions.
- Whisper: A model that can convert audio input into text with high accuracy.
- Embeddings: A set of models capable of converting text into numerical representations.
- Moderation: A fine-tuned model capable of detecting if text may be sensitive or unsafe.
- Codex: A set of models capable of understanding and generating code, including translating natural language into code.

4.4: API usage vs. web interface

GPT models can be accessed using the OpenAI API or the web interface.

The use of APIs versus web interfaces represents two different approaches to interact with services or applications.

Web interfaces are often geared towards end-users and provide a graphical interface that allows users to interact with a service or application through a web browser. This makes the usage of the service more intuitive for non-technical users. When we talk about web interfaces, we are referring to applications like ChatGPT that offer a web interface to interact with GPT-3.5 and GPT-4 or even the Playground[10], a web interface provided by OpenAI to interact with different models and explore their capabilities.

On the other hand, APIs are designed to be used by applications and developers. They enable programmatic communication between different services or software components. For example, a developer can use an API to query a specific model and retrieve the results in their application or integrate the model into their own service or application. Applications like copy.ai or Jasper are examples of web interfaces that use the OpenAI API to provide text generation services to their users through a web interface.

4.5: Tokens

GPT models process text in chunks called tokens. Tokens represent frequently occurring character sequences and they are different from words.

For example, the string "Building a ChatBot" can be broken down into 3 words "Building", "a" and "ChatBot" but when we tokenize it, it is broken down into 4 tokens "Building", " a", " Chat" and "Bot".

It is worth noting that in a sentence, the first token of each word (except the first word) typically starts with a space. In the previous example, " a" and " Chat" are the first tokens of the words "a" and "ChatBot" respectively and both tokens start with a space.

---

[10]https://platform.openai.com/playground

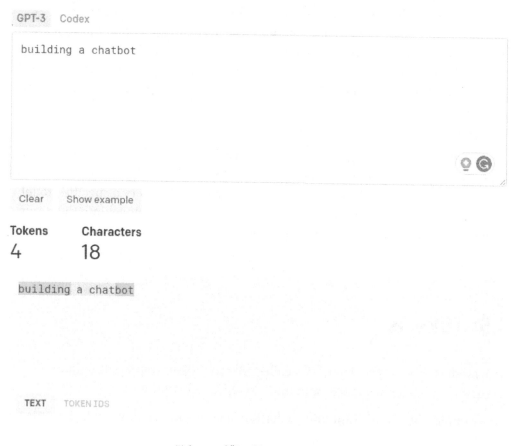

Tokens of "Building a ChatBot"

OpenAI provides a tokenizer tool[11] that allows testing specific strings and seeing how they are translated into tokens.

As a general rule, it is estimated that 1 token corresponds to approximately 4 characters or 0.75 words for English text. This could be different for other languages.

One limitation to keep in mind is that for a GPT model, the combination of the prompt and the generated output should not exceed the model's maximum context length.

The maximum context lengths for each GPT model can be found in the models index[12] provided by OpenAI.

---

[11]https://platform.openai.com/tokenizer
[12]https://platform.openai.com/docs/models/overview

GPT-4 has a max of 8192 tokens by default while GPT-3.5-turbo has 4096 tokens by default.

When using ChatGPT, the maximum context depends on the model you are using. For example, if you are using GPT-4 as your model, the maximum context length is 8192 tokens. This means you can use up to 8192 tokens in your prompt and generated output combined.

This token limitation explains why ChatGPT will sometimes generate a shorter response than expected or cut off the end of a sentence.

> ℹ️ Tokens are important to understand even if you are not a developer. This will help you understand how GPT models process text and how to use them effectively. It will also open your eyes to the real costs associated with using GPT models whether you are using them in your own application or through a service like WriteSonic or Copy.ai.

4.6: Costs, tokens and initial prompts: how to calculate the cost of using a model

If you're paying for monthly access to a ChatGPT, the cost of using the model is fixed. However, if you're using a GPT model through an API, the cost of using the model is based mainly on the number of tokens generated.

This means that the longer the prompt and the generated output, the higher the cost of the API call.

Here's how it generally works:

- **Number of tokens**: When you send text to the API, it is divided into tokens. This includes both the input text (prompt) and the generated response.

For example, if my prompt is "What is the capital of Argentina?" and the response is "Buenos Aires", the total number of tokens used is 11 including spaces: 7 for the prompt and 3 for the response.

- **Cost per token**: The API will typically have a fixed cost per token depending on the model you are using. If you are calling "gpt-4", the cost is $0.03 / 1K tokens and if you are using "gpt-4-32k" the cost is $0.06 / 1K tokens. For other models, refer to the models pricing page[13] provided by OpenAI.

To do some math, let's suppose you are using the "gpt-4" model (the cost per 1k token is $0.03). Your prompt and answer use 11 tokens. The total cost of the API call would be 11 * $0.03 / 1k = $0.00033.

If you are using a SaaS solution like Jasper, the cost of using the model is typically a fixed monthly fee with a certain number of tokens included. The monthly fee is calculated based on the number of tokens included, the cost per token and the SaaS provider's profit margin.

4.7: Prompting: how does it work?

A "prompt" refers to a text input that is provided to a language model with the goal of generating a response or output.

These are the details about the different facets of prompts:

Response trigger: The prompt acts like a trigger for the language model. By receiving the prompt, the model uses its knowledge and internal structure to generate an appropriate response. For example, giving a model the prompt "What is the capital of France?" could generate the response "Paris."

```
Prompt: What is the capital of Sweden?
Response: Stockholm
```

Basically, the model, always try to provide a completion to the prompt based on the prompt itself, the context of the conversation, the knowledge it has learned from the training data and the probability of the next word. For each token in the input, the model calculates the probability distribution of what the next token should be. It assigns higher probabilities to tokens that are more likely to follow the context given. The model then generates text by selecting the token with the

---

[13]https://openai.com/pricing#language-models

highest probability as the next word. This process is repeated until the desired length or completion is reached.

Format: Prompts can vary in length and complexity. They can be as simple as a word or a sentence, or as complex as a paragraph or more. In addition, prompts can include specific formatting, such as lists or headers, to guide the model's output.

Example:

```
Create a list of unhealthy products that should not be bought at the su\
permarket.


I -
```

Using the example above, we can see that the prompt is a simple sentence that includes a list header (I -). The model will use this information to generate a list of unhealthy products.

Example of generated output:

```
I - Canned foods
II - Processed meats
III - Sugary drinks
IV - Frozen foods
V - Snacks
```

If the prompt was:

```
Create a list of unhealthy products that should not be bought at the su\
permarket.


1 -
```

The generated output would be:

```
1 - Canned foods
2 - Processed meats
...
```

Context: In some cases, additional context can be provided in the prompt to help the model better understand the request.

```
Prompt: How many legs does it have?
Response: To answer the question "How many legs does it have?", it is n\
ecessary to know which animal you are referring to.
```

```
Prompt: I have a dog.
Response: A dog has 4 legs.
```

Another example where the user wants to get a list of tech brands but AI was not provided enough context and understood that the user wants to get a list of fruits.

```
Prompt: Continue adding elements to the following list:

"""
apple,
"""
```

```
Response:
banana, cherry, grape, orange, pear, pineapple, strawberry, watermelon
```

To provide a better context, adding another element to the list with the name of a tech brand will help AI understand that the user wants to get a list of tech brands and not fruits.

Prompt: Continue adding elements to the following list:

"""

apple, samsung,

"""

Response:
apple, samsung, acer, asus, dell, hp, huawei, lenovo, lg, microsoft, ms\
i, nokia, oppo, razer, sony, xiaomi

Conversational interaction: Prompts can be used in a conversational setting. This means that you can have a series of prompts and responses that simulate a conversation with the model.

Prompt: Hello, how are you?
Response: I'm fine, thank you. And you?
Prompt: I'm fine too. What did you do today?
Response: ..

Instructions: Prompts can also include instructions for the model. For example, a prompt could say "Write a 500-word essay about Carthage and Rome" to give the model specific instructions on the length and topic of the output.

Prompt: Write a 500-word essay about Carthage and Rome.
Response: Carthage and Rome: An Epic Rivalry of Antiquity

In the annals of history, few rivalries have had as profound an impact \
on the course of civilization as that of Carthage and Rome. Both empire
s, boasting vast territories and immense power, were destined to clash
in the Mediterranean for supremacy. This confrontation, often romantici
zed but undeniably brutal, would determine the trajectory of the Wester
n world for centuries to come.

...

Usage in model training: When training language models, prompts are often used in combination with example responses to teach the model how to correctly respond to different inputs.

Limitations; It is worth noting that language models have limitations regarding the length of prompts. Models such as GPT have a maximum context length, and if a prompt is too long, it may be necessary to truncate or summarize it.

Some "hacks" could be helpful to overcome this limitation. For example, you can split a long prompt into multiple prompts and concatenate the generated responses to get a longer response.

```
Prompt: I'm going to share with you a very long text split into multipl\
e prompts. Every part of the text will end with an "END PART" message.
You can use this  to understand where a part ends and where the next pa
rt begins. When you see the "END PART" message, reply with "NEXT PART P
LEASE" until you see "END ALL".
"END ALL" means that you have reached the end of the text. You can now \
reply with "END ALL" to confirm that you have read the entire text.
Are you ready?
```

Costs associated with API calls and prompts: When using LLMs like GPT-4 via an API, the number of tokens in the prompt affects the cost of the API call, as providers typically charge based on the number of tokens processed.

All of the above are some of the most common facets of prompts. However, there are many other facets that can be explored and we are going to discuss them in the next sections.

4.8: Probability and sampling: at the heart of GPT

GPT learns patterns and structures in text data. When you input a prompt or a starting sentence to the model, it uses its training to generate the next word or words.

The model is trained on a large dataset of text, such as books, articles, and web-sites. It learns the statistical relationships between words and the context in which they appear. Using its data the model looks for patterns and tries to predict the most likely word to come next based on the input it has received.

To generate words, the model uses a technique called "probability sampling." It assigns probabilities to different words based on their likelihood to appear in a given context. The model then selects the word with the highest probability or samples from a distribution of likely words based on parameters like temperature or top-p.

For example, if the prompt is "The weather is", the model might assign high probabilities to words like "sunny," "cloudy," or "rainy" based on what it has learned from the training data and based on the global context of the conversation. It then generates the word that has the highest probability or samples a word from the distribution to complete the sentence.

This is a simplified explanation of how generative language models work, other factors such as how the model is trained to interact with the prompt and the context of the conversation also play a role in the generation of text.

In reality, the model does not have real understanding or knowledge like a human does. It is all about building statistical relationships between words and contexts.

4.9: Understanding the API parameters

Understanding API parameters can give you a better idea of how the model works behind the scenes and how you can use it in conjunction with prompts to generate better results.

Web interface like ChatGPT, are usually designed to be easy to use and you don't have the ability to directly modify the internal parameters of my model, such as temperature.

There are some workarounds to this limitation, such as describing the desired behavior in the prompt:

```
Prompt: Write a poem about quantum physics. Be more creative.
Prompt: Write a poem about quantum physics. Only use simple words.
Prompt: Write a poem about quantum physics. Use a diverse vocabulary.
...
```

On the other hand, developers who use the OpenAI API have the option to adjust certain parameters, including temperature, when integrating language models like GPT into their applications.

Understanding and adjusting API parameters offers multiple advantages. By mastering these parameters, you not only gain insights into why the model produces certain responses but also grasp the delicate balance between coherence and diversity. This understanding allows for more effective interactions, enabling users to craft prompts or conversation styles. Moreover, it provides guidance for generating content; a deep awareness of how parameters influence outcomes allows users to better structure prompts or directions.

Here is a list of the most common parameters you may come across:

- Temperature
- Top-p
- Top-k
- Sequence length (max_tokens)
- Number of responses (n)
- Presence penalty (presence_penalty)
- Frequency penalty (frequency_penalty)
- Best of (best_of)

4.9.1: Temperature

This controls the degree of variability in responses. A higher temperature makes responses more diverse but potentially less coherent, while a lower temperature makes responses more deterministic and focused. A higher temperature may lead to hallucinations when the response should be deterministic.

4.9.2: Top-p

The "top-p" parameter, also known as "nucleus sampling," is a technique used in text generation models like GPT to control the diversity of generated responses. It allows for selecting from the most probable words while limiting the selection to a subset of words whose cumulative probability exceeds a certain threshold.

In practice, let's say we use a GPT model to generate a sequence of words from a given context. The "top-p" parameter comes into play by selecting words from the most probable ones until the cumulative probability reaches the defined threshold. This way, only the most probable words up to that point are considered, reducing the pool of choices and introducing diversity in the generated responses.

For example, if we set a threshold of 0.8 with the "top-p" parameter, it means only words with a cumulative probability reaching 80% will be considered. Less probable words will be eliminated, allowing for more targeted and coherent responses while maintaining some variety.

Here is an example of using the "top-p" parameter to generate a sentence:

Context: What is the best restaurant in town according to the reviews?"

- Without "top-p":

Response: The best restaurant in town is Restaurant A. It offers delici\ ous cuisine and exceptional service. The reviews love it!

- With "top-p" (threshold of 0.8):

Response: The best restaurant in town is undoubtedly Restaurant A. It's\ incredibly popular and highly appreciated by the critics.

In this example, the "top-p" parameter helped generate a more focused response by using only the most probable words, while still maintaining some variety in the generated response.

It is recommended not to use top-p together with temperature and choose one or the other.

4.9.3: Top-k

The "top-k" parameter is a technique used in text generation models to control the number of possible choices when selecting the next words in a generated sequence. It limits the pool of candidate tokens to the k most probable tokens at each generation step.

Specifically, the "top-k" parameter specifies the maximum number of tokens to consider at each generation step based on their probability. Tokens are ranked in descending order of probability, and only the top k most probable tokens are taken into account. Less probable tokens are, therefore, excluded from the pool of choices.

By using the "top-k" parameter, you can control the diversity of generated responses. A lower value of k would make the response more deterministic and coherent while a higher value of k would make responses more diverse but potentially less coherent.

Experimenting with and adjusting the "top-k" parameter can help you achieve better results.

4.9.4: Sequence length (max_tokens)

The sequence length refers to the number of tokens generated by the model. For example, if you instruct the model a sequence of 10 tokens, the model will simply generate 10 tokens based on the given context.

If you want to generate longer responses, you can increase the sequence length. Conversely, if you want shorter responses, you can decrease the sequence length.

🛈 The sequence length can also impact the cost of the API call.

4.9.5: Presence penalty (presence_penalty)

The presence penalty parameter ranges from -2.0 to 2.0. Positive values of this parameter will penalize tokens based on their presence (i.e., if they have appeared even once) in the generated text so far. This encourages the model to introduce new tokens, which can help the response cover new topics.

In contrast, a negative presence penalty might encourage the model to stick closer to tokens it has already introduced.

Setting a high presence penalty can lead to more varied responses, but too high a value might result in less coherent outputs as the model tries to avoid tokens it has already used.

4.9.6: Frequency penalty (frequency_penalty)

The frequency penalty parameter also ranges from -2.0 to 2.0. Positive values penalize tokens based on how frequently they have appeared in the generated text. This means a token that has been used multiple times will be penalized more heavily than a token that has appeared only once. The aim here is to discourage excessive repetition.

On the other hand, negative values would do the opposite and might encourage the model to repeat tokens it has used more frequently.

The purpose of the frequency penalty is to ensure diversity in the generated responses and prevent overuse of certain phrases or words. Using this penalty can help achieve more varied and dynamic outputs from the text generation model.

In summary, while both parameters control repetition in their own ways, the presence penalty is about whether a token has appeared at all, and the frequency penalty concerns how often a token has appeared. Adjusting these parameters requires a balance depending on the desired outcome and context of the application.

The presence penalty penalizes a token if it has appeared at all, while the frequency penalty penalizes a token based on how often it has appeared.

4.9.7: Number of responses (n)

The number of responses refers to the number of responses generated by the model. For example, if you generate 3 responses, the model will generate 3 responses based on the given context.

If you want to generate 10 responses, set the number of responses to 10 and if you want to generate a single response, you set the number of responses to 1 (default).

The number of responses can also impact the cost of the API call.

4.9.8: Best of (best_of)

The "best_of" option is used for optimal completions and returns the "best" completion (the one with the highest log-probability per token).

When used together with the "n" parameter (number of responses), "best_of" controls the number of candidate completions, and "n" specifies how many completions will be returned. It is important to note that the value of "best_of" should be greater than "n".

In practice, if you set "best_of" to 10 and "n" to 3, the model will generate 10 candidate completions and return the 3 best ones based on their log-probability per token. This allows for choosing from a larger set of generated completions and selecting the ones considered the "best" in terms of quality and coherence.

Using the "best_of" option with "n" can be useful when you want to obtain multiple high-quality results from a larger set of generated completions. This allows for selecting the most optimal responses and better controlling the quality of the returned results.

4.10: OpenAI official examples

OpenAI has created a list of examples to illustrate the capabilities of GPT models. You can find this list on the official OpenAI website[14].

These examples are a great way to get started with prompting. You can use them as a starting point for your own prompts and adjust them according to your needs.

4.11: Using the API without coding

Using OpenAI playground[15], you can test the API without writing any code. This is a great way to get started with it and explore its capabilities.

You can not only write prompts and generate text but also adjust the parameters and see how they impact the results. The parameters can be adjusted using the form on the right side of the playground.

---

[14]https://platform.openai.com/examples
[15]https://platform.openai.com/playground

The playground also allows you to see the code used to generate the results. This can be useful if you want to use the API in your own code.

On the right side of the playground, you have 4 modes: "Complete", "Chat", "Insert" and "Edit". Each mode has a different purpose and can be used for different tasks.

For example, the "Complete" mode is used for generating text based on a given prompt, while the "Chat" mode is used for generating a conversation between two speakers (typically a human and an AI).

Each mode needs a different prompt format. For example, the "Complete" mode requires a single prompt, while the "Chat" mode requires the "system" prompt and the "user" prompt.

The playground also allows you to save your prompts and results. This can be useful if you want to save your work and come back to it later. It is also possible to share your prompts and results with others.

For example, the insertion mode is used to insert text into an existing document and this is an example of a prompt for the insertion mode:

```
As the sun set, [insert] with a touch of enchantment.
```

The prompt is incomplete and the model will complete it by generating the missing part. The result will be a complete sentence that makes sense in the context of the prompt.

This is an example of a result generated by the model:

```
As the sun set, a crowd gathered outside the building's entrance. Some \
of them brought firewood and logs. Eventually, the flame of hope lit up
 the foggy night sky, lending the scene with a touch of enchantment.
```

If you want to see the code used to generate the result, you can click on the "View code" button on the right side of the playground.

This is an example of the code used to generate the result:

```
import os
import openai

openai.api_key = os.getenv("OPENAI_API_KEY")

response = openai.Completion.create(
  model="text-davinci-003",
  prompt="As the sun set, ",
  suffix=" with a touch of enchantment.",
  temperature=1,
  max_tokens=256,
  top_p=1,
  frequency_penalty=0,
  presence_penalty=0
)
```

This snippet of code can be used to generate the same result in your own code. Remember that you don't need to use the same parameters. You can adjust the parameters according to your specific needs and preferences.

Let's explore each endpoint in more detail.

4.12: Completion (deprecated)

The completion endpoint[16] is used for generating text based on a given prompt. This is the most basic endpoint and it is used for generating text based on a single prompt.

Example of a prompt:

```
Once upon a time
```

Another example:

---

[16]https://platform.openai.com/playground/?mode=complete

Introduction

Discover the benefits of mindfulness meditation, a practice that transp\
orts you to a state of Zen and tranquility. Meditation, with its power
of deep relaxation, is often likened to a clear blue sky. By engaging i
n this regular practice, you cultivate mindful attention to the present
 moment. Mindfulness meditation allows you to connect with yourself, ca
lm the mental chatter, and find inner balance. Dive into this ocean of
serenity and let meditation guide you to a state of calm and equilibriu
m.

How to Practice

Another example showing the use of the "stop" parameter:

The list of things I should not buy at the grocery store:

1.

If you want to have only 5 items in the list, you can use the "stop" parameter to
stop the generation after the 6th item. You should set the "stop" parameter to "6."
(note the dot at the end).

Using the stop parameter

When the parameter is encountered, the API returns the generated responses up
to this point. This can be useful for generating shorter responses or limiting the
number of answers.

4.13: Chat

The chat endpoint[17] is used for generating a conversation between two speakers. This endpoint uses two initial prompts: the "system" prompt (optional) and the "user" prompt (required).

Example of a "system" prompt:

```
You are a helpful assistant helping users with their questions about di\
et and nutrition. You are talking to a person who wants to build muscle
 and lose fat.
```

Remember that setting a role for AI is useful to help it understand the context of the conversation.

4.14: Insert (deprecated)

As explained earlier, the insert endpoint[18] is used to insert text into an existing document. This endpoint requires a text prompt and a "insert" parameter.

Example of a prompt:

```
When the [insert] is over, the world will be a better place.
```

The prompt is incomplete and the model will complete it by generating the missing part. The result will be a complete sentence that makes sense in the context of the prompt. The prompt is limited to 1 insert parameter.

4.15: Edit (deprecated)

The edit endpoint[19] is used to edit an existing text. This endpoint requires two prompts:

---

[17]https://platform.openai.com/playground/?mode=chat
[18]https://platform.openai.com/playground/?mode=insert
[19]https://platform.openai.com/playground/?mode=edit

- The input prompt
- The instruction prompt

The first prompt is used to provide the initial text and the second prompt is used to provide the instructions for editing the text.

Example of an input prompt:

```
When the moon sets, all the birds fly back to their nests.
```

Example of an instruction prompt:

```
Delete the word "moon" and replace it with "sun". Delete the word "fly"\
 and replace it with "return".
```

Example of a result:

```
When the sun sets, all the birds return to their nests.
```

The model will edit the text according to the instructions provided in the instruction prompt.

Instructions can be used to perform various operations on the text. For example, you can use instructions to delete, replace or insert text and even to change the formatting of the text or translate it into another language.

```
Input: I have 2 apples and 3 oranges. My friend has 1 apple and 2 orang\
es.
User: Format the input as a JSON object
AI: {
  "I": {
    "apples": 2,
    "oranges": 3
  },
  "My friend": {
    "apples": 1,
    "oranges": 2
  }
}
```

5: Setting up the environment

5.1: Choosing the model

Since OpenAI GPT models are the most popular and widely used models and because they are easily accessible through the OpenAI API, we are going to use them in this guide. However, to apply the concepts and techniques discussed in this guide to other models, you can use the same approach in almost all cases without any major changes.

Our goal is understanding the concepts and techniques behind prompt engineering and how to apply them to different models. We are not going to focus on the technical details of each model.

5.2: Choosing the programming language

OpenAI API supports Python and Node.js officially[20]. Azure OpenAI libraries[21] are available for .NET, Java, JavaScript, and Go. Other community libraries[22] are available for other languages as well (e.g. Rust, PHP, etc.).

We are going to use Python for this guide as it is the most popular language for AI and machine learning. It is also easy to get started with Python even if you are not a Python developer.

5.3: Installing the prerequisites

We are going to create a Python virtual environment for this guide to avoid any conflicts with other Python projects on your machine.

---

[20]https://platform.openai.com/docs/libraries/libraries
[21]https://platform.openai.com/docs/libraries/azure-openai-libraries
[22]https://platform.openai.com/docs/libraries/community-libraries

To create a virtual environment, you can use Virtualenv, Virtualenvwrapper, or other tools. We are going to use Virtualenvwrapper[23] for this guide.

Start by installing pip and virtualenvwrapper:

```
sudo apt install python3-pip
sudo pip3 install virtualenvwrapper
```

If you are using Windows, you can install pip and virtualenvwrapper using Chocolatey[24]:

```
choco install pip
pip install virtualenvwrapper-win
```

However, I recommend using an Ubuntu virtual machine on Windows using Multipass[25] or any other virtualization tool. Alternatively, you can use a cloud like DigitalOcean or AWS.

We are also going to use Python 3.9 for our development environment. You should have Python 3.9 installed, follow this link to install Python 3.9[26].

Next, create a virtual environment called pe (short for prompt engineering) using Python 3.9:

```
mkvirtualenv pe --python=$(which python3.9)
```

On windows, you can use the following command:

```
mkvirtualenv pe --python=<path to python.exe>
```

Make sure to replace <path to python.exe> with the actual path to python.exe on your machine.

After creating the virtual environment, it will be activated automatically. Make sure that you are using Python 3.9:

---

[23]https://github.com/python-virtualenvwrapper/virtualenvwrapper
[24]https://chocolatey.org/
[25]https://multipass.run/
[26]https://www.python.org/downloads/

```
python --version
```

5.4: Installing the OpenAI Python library

The OpenAI Python library is available on PyPI[27]. You can install it using pip:

```
pip install openai==0.27.8
```

5.5: Getting an OpenAI API key

To use the OpenAI API, you need to get an API key. You can get one by signing up for OpenAI[28] then creating a new API key here[29].

Note that the usage of the API is paid. However for this guide, the total cost will not exceed $10. It's probably half of that.

Don't forget to export the API key as an environment variable:

```
export OPENAI_API_KEY=<your API key>
```

5.6: A hello world example

Let's start by creating a simple Python script to test our installation.

In the past, OpenAI API had endpoints like "Completion" and "Edit" that are now deprecated. The new API has a single endpoint called "ChatCompletion" that can be used for all most cases. The company recommends that users adopt the Chat Completions API, which has proven to be powerful and handles the majority of use cases with higher flexibility and specificity. This is the endpoint that we are going to use in this example.

Create a file called app.py and add the following code:

---

[27]https://pypi.org/project/openai/
[28]https://platform.openai.com/
[29]https://platform.openai.com/account/api-keys

```python
# Import necessary libraries
import os          # Used for accessing environment variables
import openai       # OpenAI's Python client library

# Retrieve the OpenAI API key from environment variables
openai.api_key = os.getenv("OPENAI_API_KEY")

# Print an initial greeting message from Felix, the chatbot
print("Felix: Hi there. I am Felix, the chatbot. How can I help you tod\
ay?")

# Get the user's message/input
user_message = input("You: ")

# Use the OpenAI API to generate a response based on the user's message
response = openai.ChatCompletion.create(
  model="gpt-3.5-turbo",   # Specify the model to be used
  messages=[
    # System message to set the behavior of the assistant
    {
      "role": "system",
      "content": "You are smart and helpful assistant."
    },
    # Initial user message (this is hardcoded and not used for any dyna\
mic interaction)
    {
      "role": "user",
      "content": "Hi there."
    },
    # Initial assistant's response to the hardcoded user message
    {
      "role": "assistant",
      "content": "Hi there. \n\nI am Felix, the chatbot.\n\nHow can I h\
elp you today?"
    },
    # Actual user's message that was inputted earlier
```

```
  {
    "role": "user",
    "content": f"{user_message}"
  },
 ],
 # Parameters to guide the generation of the response
 temperature=1,            # Controls randomness. Higher values make out\
put more random.
 max_tokens=256,           # Maximum number of tokens (words/characters)\
 in the response
 top_p=1,                  # Nucleus sampling parameter. Controls divers\
ity of the output.
 frequency_penalty=0,      # Controls the penalty for using frequent tok\
ens. 0 means no penalty.
 presence_penalty=0        # Controls the penalty for using new tokens. \
0 means no penalty.
)

# Try to print the generated response
try:
  print("Felix: " + response.choices[0].message.content)
# If there's an error (e.g., API error, network issues), print an error\
 message
except:
  print("Felix: Sorry, a problem occured. Please try again later.")
```

This code sets up a simple chatbot interaction using the OpenAI API. The user provides a message, and the chatbot (named Felix) responds based on the given message and the previous hardcoded conversation context. If there's any issue with the API call, it gracefully handles the error and informs the user.

5.7: Interactive prompting

In order to make the chatbot interactive, we will use click to create a command-line interface (CLI) for the chatbot. Click[30] is a third-party Python package for creating command line interfaces in a composable way with as little code as necessary. It's the "Command Line Interface Creation Kit".

Install click using pip:

```
pip install click==8.1.7
```

Next, update the code in app.py to use click:

```python
import os
import openai
import click


openai.api_key = os.getenv("OPENAI_API_KEY")

@click.command()
def chat_with_felix():
    """Chat with Felix, the chatbot."""
    print("Felix: Hi there. I am Felix, the chatbot. How can I help you\
 today?")

    while True:  # This will keep the chat session active
        message = input("You: ")

        # Exit the loop (and the program) if the user types 'exit' or '\
quit'
        if message.lower() in ['exit', 'quit']:
            print("Felix: Goodbye!")
            break
```

---

[30]https://palletsprojects.com/p/click/

```python
    response = openai.ChatCompletion.create(
        model="gpt-3.5-turbo",
        messages=[
            {"role": "system", "content": "You are smart and helpfu\
l assistant."},
            {"role": "user", "content": "Hi there."},
            {"role": "assistant", "content": "Hi there. \n\nI am Fe\
lix, the chatbot.\n\nHow can I help you today?"},
            {"role": "user", "content": f"{message}"},
        ],
        temperature=1,
        max_tokens=256,
        top_p=1,
        frequency_penalty=0,
        presence_penalty=0
    )

    try:
        print("Felix:", response.choices[0].message.content)
    except:
        print("Felix: Sorry, a problem occurred. Please try again l\
ater.")

if __name__ == '__main__':
    chat_with_felix()
```

Execute the script using the following command:

```
python app.py
```

Notice that the chatbot is now interactive. You can type a message and the chatbot will respond to it. You can also type "exit" or "quit" to exit the interaction.

5.8: Interactive prompting with mutliline prompt

In some cases, we will use a prompt like the following:

Write a story about a robot that is trying to learn how to be a human.

The robot is called Tobor. Once Tobor acquired the ability to speak, he\
 started to learn how to be a human. He started by learning how to thin
k and develop a creative imagination.

In this case, we need to accept multiline input from the user. We can do that using the following code:

```
import os
import openai
import click


openai.api_key = os.getenv("OPENAI_API_KEY")

@click.command()
def chat_with_felix():
    """Chat with Felix, the chatbot."""
    print("Felix: Hi there. I am Felix, the chatbot. How can I help you\
 today?")

    while True:  # This will keep the chat session active
        print("You: (Type your message. When done, type 'END' on a new \
line)")
        lines = []
        while True:
            line = input()
            if line == "END":
                break
            lines.append(line)
```

```python
        message = '\n'.join(lines)

        # Exit the loop (and the program) if the user types 'exit' or '\
quit'
        if message.lower() in ['exit', 'quit']:
            print("Felix: Goodbye!")
            break

        response = openai.ChatCompletion.create(
            model="gpt-3.5-turbo",
            messages=[
                {"role": "system", "content": "You are smart and helpfu\
l assistant."},
                {"role": "user", "content": "Hi there."},
                {"role": "assistant", "content": "Hi there. \n\nI am Fe\
lix, the chatbot.\n\nHow can I help you today?"},
                {"role": "user", "content": f"{message}"},
            ],
            temperature=1,
            max_tokens=256,
            top_p=1,
            frequency_penalty=0,
            presence_penalty=0
        )

        try:
            print("Felix:", response.choices[0].message.content)
        except:
            print("Felix: Sorry, a problem occurred. Please try again l\
ater.")

if __name__ == '__main__':
    chat_with_felix()
```

6: Few-shot Learning and Chain of Thought

6.1: What is few-shot learning?

Few-shot learning, sometimes referred to as low-shot learning, is a method that allows models to make accurate predictions with only a few examples, reducing data collection and computation efforts and costs. This technique has been applied in various fields such as:

- Computer vision (character recognition, object tracking, classification)
- NLP (text completion, translation, classification)
- Audio processing (voice cloning, conversion)

6.2: Zero-shot vs few-shot learning

Large language models such as GPT-4, PaLM 2, Llama 2 and others were trained on massive datasets and they can perform well on a wide range of tasks. Therfore, they are usually prompted without any examples. This is what we call zero-shot learning. However, when the task is complex, the model needs to be trained on a few examples to perform well and here comes the few-shot learning technique.

Still, the quality of your prompt and using the best practices can help you achieve better results with zero-shot learning (context, coherence, persona..etc).

In fact, zero-shot learning is the preferred method for most cases. It's faster and easier.

6.3: Approaches to few-shot learning

There are different approaches to few-shot learning and they include using:

6.3.1: Prior knowledge about similarity

During training, we develop embeddings that can distinguish between different classes, even if they haven't been seen before.

Think of this like teaching a AI to recognize the difference between cats and dogs by showing it many pictures. Even if later it sees a breed of cat or dog it hasn't seen before, it can still guess correctly because it has learned the general idea of what makes a cat different from a dog. This is a bit like a game where you match similar items, and the AI gets better at it over time.

6.3.2: Prior knowledge about learning

We leverage pre-existing knowledge to guide the learning algorithm in selecting parameters that not only fit the data well but also generalize effectively. This helps in preventing overfitting, especially when working with limited data.

Imagine you're teaching someone to ride a scooter. Instead of starting from scratch, if they've ridden a bike before, you'd use that knowledge to help them learn faster. In the same way, when teaching an AI, we use what it already knows to help it learn new things without making common mistakes.

6.3.3: Prior knowledge of data

By harnessing our understanding of the data's inherent structure and variations, we can effectively train AI even when provided with only a handful of examples. This knowledge acts as a foundation for more efficient learning.

Let's say you're trying to teach someone about different types of fruits. If they already know about apples and oranges, you can use that knowledge to explain a tangerine (it's like a small orange!). In the same fashion, when teaching an AI, if it knows a bit about the type of information (or data) you're giving it, it can learn new things more easily.

6.4: Examples of few-shot learning

Let's start with this simple example:

```python
import os
import openai
import click

openai.api_key = os.getenv("OPENAI_API_KEY")

@click.command()
def chat_with_felix():
    """Chat with Felix, the chatbot."""
    print("Felix: Hi there. I am Felix, the chatbot. Let's play a game.\
 Give me a number and I'll tell you if it's even or odd.")

    while True:
        message = input("You: ")

        if message.lower() in ['exit', 'quit']:
            print("Felix: Goodbye!")
            break

        response = openai.ChatCompletion.create(
            model="gpt-3.5-turbo",
            messages=[
                {"role": "system", "content": "You are a smart and help\
ful assistant."},

                {"role": "user", "content": "1"},
                {"role": "assistant", "content": "1 is an odd number be\
cause it is not divisible by 2."},

                {"role": "user", "content": "2"},
                {"role": "assistant", "content": "2 is an even number b\
```

```
ecause it is divisible by 2."},

            {"role": "user", "content": "3"},
            {"role": "assistant", "content": "3 is an odd number be\
cause it is not divisible by 2."},

            {"role": "user", "content": f"{message}"},
        ],
        temperature=1,
        max_tokens=256,
        top_p=1,
        frequency_penalty=0,
        presence_penalty=0
    )

    try:
        print("Felix:", response.choices[0].message.content)
    except:
        print("Felix: Sorry, a problem occurred. Please try again l\
ater.")


if __name__ == '__main__':
    chat_with_felix()
```

Interacting with the AI:

```
Felix: Hi there. I am Felix, the chatbot. Let's play a game. Give me a \
number and I'll tell you if it's even or odd.
You: 6
exitFelix: 6 is an even number because it is divisible by 2.
You:
Felix: Goodbye!
```

In this example, we are using a few-shot learning technique to teach the AI to recognize even and odd numbers and answer accordingly in a custom way.

Another example is the following:

```python
import os
import openai
import click

openai.api_key = os.getenv("OPENAI_API_KEY")

@click.command()
def chat_with_felix():
    """Chat with Felix, the chatbot."""
    print("Felix: Hi there. I am Felix, the chatbot. Let's play a game.\
 Name an animal, and I'll tell you if it's a mammal or not.")

    while True:
        message = input("You: ")

        if message.lower() in ['exit', 'quit']:
            print("Felix: Goodbye!")
            break

        response = openai.ChatCompletion.create(
            model="gpt-3.5-turbo",
            messages=[
                {"role": "system", "content": "You are a smart and help\
ful assistant."},

                {"role": "user", "content": "dog"},
                {"role": "assistant", "content": "A dog is a mammal bec\
ause it gives birth to live young and has fur."},

                {"role": "user", "content": "fish"},
                {"role": "assistant", "content": "A fish is not a mamma\
l because it lays eggs and lives in water."},

                {"role": "user", "content": f"{message}"},
            ],
            temperature=1,
```

```
        max_tokens=256,
        top_p=1,
        frequency_penalty=0,
        presence_penalty=0
    )

    try:
        print("Felix:", response.choices[0].message.content)
    except:
        print("Felix: Sorry, a problem occurred. Please try again l\
ater.")

if __name__ == '__main__':
    chat_with_felix()
```

Interacting with the AI:

```
Felix: Hi there. I am Felix, the chatbot. Let's play a game. Name an an\
imal, and I'll tell you if it's a mammal or not.
You: cow
exit
Felix: A cow is also a mammal. It is a large domesticated ungulate anim\
al that is raised as livestock for meat, milk, and other dairy products
. Cows give birth to live young and produce milk to feed their offsprin
g.
You: Felix: Goodbye!
```

6.5: Limitations of few-shot learning

Let's consider an example where we want the AI to answer with "X" if the input is
an odd number and "Y" if the input is an even number. We can use the following
code that uses a few-shot learning technique:

```python
import os
import openai
import click

openai.api_key = os.getenv("OPENAI_API_KEY")

@click.command()
def chat_with_felix():
    """Chat with Felix, the chatbot."""
    print("Felix: Hi there. I am Felix, the chatbot. Let's play a game.\
")

    while True:
        message = input("You: ")

        if message.lower() in ['exit', 'quit']:
            print("Felix: Goodbye!")
            break

        response = openai.ChatCompletion.create(
            model="gpt-3.5-turbo",
            messages=[
                {"role": "system", "content": "You are a smart and help\
ful assistant."},

                {"role": "user", "content": "1"},
                {"role": "assistant", "content": "X"},

                {"role": "user", "content": "2"},
                {"role": "assistant", "content": "Y"},

                {"role": "user", "content": f"{message}"},
            ],
            temperature=1,
            max_tokens=256,
            top_p=1,
```

```
        frequency_penalty=0,
        presence_penalty=0
    )

    try:
        print("Felix:", response.choices[0].message.content)
    except:
        print("Felix: Sorry, a problem occurred. Please try again l\
ater.")


if __name__ == '__main__':
    chat_with_felix()
```

This is an execution example:

```
Felix: Hi there. I am Felix, the chatbot. Let's play a game.
You: 1
Felix: X
You: 2
Felix: I'm sorry, but I'm not sure what you're referring to with "2." C\
ould you please provide more context or clarify your question?
You: 3
Felix: Z
You: 4
Felix: Z
You: 5
Felix: Z
```

This is not the expected behavior! In order to solve this problem, we can use a different prompt, such as the following:

```python
import os
import openai
import click

openai.api_key = os.getenv("OPENAI_API_KEY")

@click.command()
def chat_with_felix():
    """Chat with Felix, the chatbot."""
    print("Felix: Hi there. I am Felix, the chatbot. Let's play a game.\
")

    while True:
        message = input("You: ")

        if message.lower() in ['exit', 'quit']:
            print("Felix: Goodbye!")
            break

        response = openai.ChatCompletion.create(
            model="gpt-3.5-turbo",
            messages=[
                {"role": "system", "content": "You are a smart and help\
ful assistant."},

                {"role": "user", "content": "1"},
                {"role": "assistant", "content": "1 is an odd number so\
 the answer is X."},

                {"role": "user", "content": "2"},
                {"role": "assistant", "content": "2 is an even number s\
o the answer is Y."},

                {"role": "user", "content": "3"},
                {"role": "assistant", "content": "3 is an odd number so\
 the answer is X."},
```

```
            {"role": "user", "content": f"{message}"},
        ],
        temperature=1,
        max_tokens=256,
        top_p=1,
        frequency_penalty=0,
        presence_penalty=0
    )

    try:
        print("Felix:", response.choices[0].message.content)
    except:
        print("Felix: Sorry, a problem occurred. Please try again l\
ater.")

if __name__ == '__main__':
    chat_with_felix()
```

This is an execution example:

```
Felix: Hi there. I am Felix, the chatbot. Let's play a game.
You: 10
Felix: 10 is an even number so the answer is Y.
You: 22
Felix: 22 is an even number so the answer is Y.
You: 44
Felix: 44 is an even number so the answer is Y.
You: 12
Felix: 12 is an even number so the answer is Y.
You: 13
Felix: 13 is an odd number so the answer is X.
You: 19
Felix: 19 is an odd number so the answer is X.
```

This is the expected behavior.

What we did to solve the problem was to provide a reasoning for the answer. This is a common technique used in few-shot learning to bypass some of the few-shot learning limitations. The few-shot learning technique can return wrong answers if the prompt especially when the problem is complex. By providing a reasoning for the answer, or what we call "Chain of Thoughts", we can help the AI to understand the problem better and provide the correct answer.

7: Chain of Thought (CoT)

According to a "When do you need Chain-of-Thought Prompting for ChatGPT?[31]" (Chen, J., Chen, L., Huang, H., & Zhou, T. (2023)), by simply adding CoT instruction, GPT-3's accuracy can be improved from 17.7% to 78.7%. This is a huge improvement but not every query needs a CoT instruction.

In fact, the CoT instruction is only needed when the query is complex and the AI needs more information to understand the problem.

CoT is a technique that allows us to provide a reasoning for the answer. This technique is used in combination with few-shot learning to bypass some of the few-shot learning limitations.

Let's use this example:

```python
import os
import openai
import click


openai.api_key = os.getenv("OPENAI_API_KEY")


@click.command()
def chat_with_felix():
    """Chat with Felix, the chatbot."""
    print("Felix: Hi there. I am Felix, the chatbot. Let's play a game.\
")

    while True:
        message = input("You: ")

        if message.lower() in ['exit', 'quit']:
            print("Felix: Goodbye!")
```

---

[31]https://arxiv.org/abs/2304.03262

```
        break

    response = openai.ChatCompletion.create(
        model="gpt-3.5-turbo",
        messages=[
            {"role": "system", "content": "You are a smart and help\
ful assistant."},
            {"role": "user", "content": f"{message}"},
        ],
        temperature=1,
        max_tokens=256,
        top_p=1,
        frequency_penalty=0,
        presence_penalty=0
    )

    try:
        print("Felix:", response.choices[0].message.content)
    except:
        print("Felix: Sorry, a problem occurred. Please try again l\
ater.")


if __name__ == '__main__':
    chat_with_felix()
```

Then ask the following question:

```
When James was 2 years old, his sister was 2*2 years old. James is now \
30 years old. How old is his sister?
```

This is how the dialog looks like:

```
Felix: Hi there. I am Felix, the chatbot. Let's play a game.
You: When James was 2 years old, his sister was 2*2 years old. James is\
 now 30 years old. How old is his sister?
Felix: If James was 2 years old, then his sister was 2*2 = 4 years old.
Since James is now 30 years old, his sister would be 30 - 2 = 28 years \
old.
```

As you can see, the answer is partially correct, which means that gpt-3.5-turbo was able to understand the age difference but didn't guess the correct age of the sister.

Even after asking a different question, the answer is still not correct:

```
Felix: Hi there. I am Felix, the chatbot. Let's play a game.
You: When Harry was 25 years old, his sister was 29 years old. Harry is\
 now 30 years old. How old is his sister?
Felix: If Harry is now 30 years old, then his sister is 29 years old, a\
ssuming their age difference remains constant.
```

A CoT instruction should improve the answer.

```python
import os
import openai
import click


openai.api_key = os.getenv("OPENAI_API_KEY")

@click.command()
def chat_with_felix():
    """Chat with Felix, the chatbot."""
    print("Felix: Hi there. I am Felix, the chatbot. Let's play a game.\
")

    while True:
        message = input("You: ")

        if message.lower() in ['exit', 'quit']:
```

```
        print("Felix: Goodbye!")
        break

    response = openai.ChatCompletion.create(
        model="gpt-3.5-turbo",
        messages=[
            {"role": "system", "content": "You are a smart and help\
ful assistant."},
            {"role": "user", "content": "When James was 2 years old\
, his sister was 2*2 years old. James is now 30 years old. How old is h
is sister?"},
            {"role": "assistant", "content": "When James was 2 year\
s old, his sister was 4 years old. There's 2 year differences between t
hem and the sister is older than James. When James is 30 years old, his
 sister should be 32 years old."},
            {"role": "user", "content": "When Harry was 25 years ol\
d, his sister was 29 years old. Harry is now 30 years old. How old is h
is sister?"},
            {"role": "assistant", "content": "When Harry was 25 yea\
rs old, his sister was 29 years old. There's 4 year differences between
 them and the sister is older than Harry. When Harry is 30 years old, h
is sister should be 34 years old."},
            {"role": "user", "content": f"{message}"},
        ],
        temperature=1,
        max_tokens=256,
        top_p=1,
        frequency_penalty=0,
        presence_penalty=0
    )

    try:
        print("Felix:", response.choices[0].message.content)
    except:
        print("Felix: Sorry, a problem occurred. Please try again l\
ater.")
```

```
if __name__ == '__main__':
    chat_with_felix()
```

When asked the following question, the answer was correct:

```
Felix: Hi there. I am Felix, the chatbot. Let's play a game.
You: When James was 50 years old, his sister was 50/2 years old. James \
is now 100 years old. How old is his sister?
Felix: When James was 50 years old, his sister was 50/2 years old, whic\
h is 25 years old. There's a 25-year difference between them and the si
ster is younger than James.

Now that James is 100 years old, his sister would be 100 - 25 = 75 year\
s old.
```

Another question to test the CoT instruction:

```
Felix: Hi there. I am Felix, the chatbot. Let's play a game.
You: When James was 10 years old, his sister was 10*3 years old. James \
is now 30 years old. How old is his sister?
Felix: When James was 10 years old, his sister was 10*3 = 30 years old.
Since then, the age difference between them remains the same.
Therefore, if James is now 30 years old, his sister would be 30 + (30-1\
0) = 50 years old.
```

Asked without any CoT instruction, the answer was wrong:

```
Felix: Hi there. I am Felix, the chatbot. Let's play a game.
You: When James was 10 years old, his sister was 10*3 years old. James \
is now 30 years old. How old is his sister?
Felix: When James was 10 years old, his sister was 10*3 = 30 years old.\
 This age difference of 30 years remains constant over time. Since Jame
s is now 30 years old, his sister would be 30 + 30 = 60 years old.
```

Some problems like symbolic and arithmetic reasoning are complex for AIs like GPT models and require a CoT instruction to help the model understand the problem better. This is because the model essentially has no idea what the problem is about, it just tries to guess the answer based on its generative capabilities and not logic.

In our example, the CoT enabled the model to break down a problem to steps that are manageable to understand. Consider this as a transparent box that allows the model to see what's inside and understand the reasoning behind the answer.

The authors of "Chain-of-Thought Prompting Elicits Reasoning in Large Language Models[32]" (Wei, J., Wang, X., Schuurmans, D., Bosma, M., Ichter, B., Xia, F., Chi, E., Le, Q., & Zhou, D. (2022)) investigated the use of the CoT method to enhance the reasoning capabilities of large language models. They demonstrated that when large models are given a few examples of this method, they naturally improve their reasoning abilities. Testing on three major language models revealed that this approach boosts performance in arithmetic, commonsense, and symbolic reasoning tasks. Notably, by using only eight examples of this method, a 540B-parameter language model achieved top accuracy on the GSM8K[33] math word problem benchmark, outperforming even a specialized GPT-3 model.

---

[32]https://arxiv.org/abs/2201.11903
[33]https://paperswithcode.com/dataset/gsm8k

8: Zero-shot CoT Prompting

Sometimes, you don't want or you simply can't provide examples for a CoT instruction. In this case, zero-shot CoT prompting could be an alternative.

Let's try this code where we don't provide any examples for the CoT instruction:

```python
import os
import openai
import click


openai.api_key = os.getenv("OPENAI_API_KEY")

@click.command()
def chat_with_felix():
    """Chat with Felix, the chatbot."""
    print("Felix: Hi there. I am Felix, the chatbot. Let's play a game.\
")

    while True:
        message = input("You: ")

        if message.lower() in ['exit', 'quit']:
            print("Felix: Goodbye!")
            break

        response = openai.ChatCompletion.create(
            model="gpt-3.5-turbo",
            messages=[
                {"role": "system", "content": "You are a smart and help\
ful assistant."},
                {"role": "user", "content": f"{message}"},
            ],
```

```
        temperature=1,
        max_tokens=256,
        top_p=1,
        frequency_penalty=0,
        presence_penalty=0
    )

    try:
        print("Felix:", response.choices[0].message.content)
    except:
        print("Felix: Sorry, a problem occurred. Please try again l\
ater.")

if __name__ == '__main__':
    chat_with_felix()
```

Now, this is the instruction that uses the zero-shot CoT prompting technique:

```
When James was 2 years old, his sister was 2*2 years old. James is now \
30 years old. How old is his sister? Think step by step (who's older, t
he age difference..etc)
```

As you can see, we added the following Think step by step (who's older, the age difference..etc) at the end of the question. This is how the dialog looks like:

```
Felix: Hi there. I am Felix, the chatbot. Let's play a game.
You: When James was 2 years old, his sister was 2*2 years old. James is\
 now 30 years old. How old is his sister? Think step by step (who's old
er, the age difference..etc)
Felix: To find out how old James's sister is, we can work through the p\
roblem step by step:

1. When James was 2 years old, his sister was 2 * 2 years old, which me\
ans his sister was 4 years old at that time.
```

```
2. This implies that James's sister is two years older than him, as she\
 was 4 years old when he was 2 years old.

3. Since James is now 30 years old, we need to account for the age diff\
erence of two years between him and his sister.

4. To calculate his sister's current age, we add the age difference to \
James's age: 30 + 2 = 32.

Therefore, James's sister is 32 years old.
```

Surprisingly, the answer is correct and the CoT instruction helped the model to understand that breaking the problem into smaller steps while taking into consideration the age difference is the right approach to solve the problem.

This approach was introduced in the paper "Large Language Models are Zero-Shot Reasoners[34]" (Kojima, T., Gu, S. S., Reid, M., Matsuo, Y., & Iwasawa, Y. (2022)). While LLMs are praised for their few-shot learning, the authors of this paper discovered that these models can also reason without any prior examples (zero-shot) by simply prompting them to "think step by step."

> we show that LLMs are decent zero-shot reasoners by simply adding "Let's think step by step" before each answer

Their method, named Zero-shot-CoT, using just this single prompt, greatly improved performance on various reasoning tasks. For instance, accuracy on the MultiArith task (collection of multi-step arithmetic problems) jumped from 17.7% to 78.7%. This approach's success across different tasks suggests that LLMs have untapped potential for zero-shot reasoning. They believe their findings emphasize the need to explore the vast knowledge within LLMs before creating specific training datasets or examples.

While this approach could help you gain some time and effort, it's not always accurate.

---

[34]https://arxiv.org/abs/2205.11916

9: Auto Chain of Thought Prompting (AutoCoT)

Large Language Models can reason through problems by breaking them down into smaller steps. This method, known as chain-of-thought (CoT) prompting, has two main approaches. The first uses a straightforward prompt like "Let's think step by step" to guide the model's thinking. The second involves manually creating demonstrations that show a question and its step-by-step reasoning. While the second approach performs better, it relies heavily on crafting these demonstrations by hand.

The authors of "Automatic Chain of Thought Prompting in Large Language Models[35]" (Zhang, Z., Zhang, A., Li, M., & Smola, A. (2022)) found that by using the "Let's think step by step" prompting approach, LLMs can generate the reasoning steps themselves, though they sometimes make errors. To improve the quality of these automatically generated steps, they sateted that it's essential to have diverse questions. They introduced an automated method, Auto-CoT, which selects diverse questions and then generates the reasoning steps. In tests with GPT-3 on ten benchmark reasoning tasks, Auto-CoT performed as well as, or better than, the manual CoT method.

Auto-CoT works using two primary steps to help a language model reason through problems:

1.Question clustering:

- This stage organizes questions from a dataset[36] into groups or "clusters" based on their similarities.
- Each question is transformed into a vector using Sentence-BERT, which captures its essence in a numerical form.

---

[35]https://arxiv.org/abs/2210.03493
[36]https://github.com/kojima-takeshi188/zero_shot_cot/tree/main/dataset

- These vectors are then grouped using the k-means clustering algorithm. Questions closer in meaning end up in the same cluster.

2.Demonstration sampling:

- For each cluster, a representative question is chosen.
- The model is then prompted to think step-by-step using the "Let's think step by step" prompt to generate a reasoning chain for that question.
- The goal is to create a demonstration that combines the question with its reasoning chain.
- There are certain criteria for selecting these demonstrations, such as the question being short (no more than 60 tokens) and the reasoning being concise (no more than 5 steps).

After these two main stages, the demonstrations are used to help the model answer test questions. The model is given all the demonstrations and then a test question to answer, using the reasoning methods it observed in the demonstrations.

The figure 4 from the paper[37] shows the Auto-CoT process. In simpler words, Auto-CoT is like teaching the model by example, but instead of humans crafting these examples, the model generates them itself, learning how to reason step-by-step.

---

[37] https://arxiv.org/pdf/2210.03493.pdf

10: Self-consistency

GPT-3.5 and similar NLP models are trained using vast text datasets, enabling them to produce relevant and logical replies based on the training examples. However, they don't understand math and logic; they just use recognized patterns to form answers. In other words, they can't explain their reasoning, they just "mixes" words to form an eloquent answer. While the Chain-of-Thought (CoT) method, which prompts the model to explain its reasoning step-by-step, has shown promise in improving reasoning, it's not foolproof. Here's why:

- Over-reliance on a single path: CoT typically uses a "greedy" approach, meaning it often sticks to the first, most obvious reasoning path it finds. This can lead to errors if that path is flawed or if there's a better solution it hasn't considered.

Imagine CoT as a hiker in a vast forest. The moment the hiker sees a path, instead of exploring the entire forest or searching for alternative routes, they immediately take the first and most obvious trail they come across. This might get them to a destination quickly, but there's no guarantee it's the best or most scenic route, and sometimes it might even lead to a dead end.

- Lack of diversity: Since CoT tends to follow a single line of reasoning, it might miss out on other valid ways to approach a problem. This can be especially limiting for complex problems where multiple perspectives are beneficial.

Still using the hiker metaphor - imagine the forest has many hidden beautiful spots scattered in different areas. Since CoT, our hiker, consistently chooses the first path they see, they might reach one spot quickly but completely miss out on the others. For a hiker who wants to truly understand and experience the richness of the forest's spots, exploring multiple trails would be far more beneficial than sticking to just one. Similarly, for complex problems, considering a range of pathways or perspectives can lead to more insightful answers.

- Not always optimal: Just because a model can explain its reasoning doesn't mean that reasoning is correct. CoT can sometimes lead to verbose or round-about explanations that sound logical but are actually based on incorrect assumptions.

It's like our hiker who, when asked why they chose a particular path, gives a lengthy description of the trail markers, the condition of the path, and the sounds of the birds they heard, making it sound like a well-thought-out decision. However, they might have missed the clear sign at the trailhead warning of a bridge out ahead or the recommendation for a more scenic route or a beautiful spot. Their explanation might sound detailed and logical, but it's rooted in overlooking critical information or misinterpreting the signs they did see.

So while CoT helps models "show their work", it doesn't guarantee that the work is always correct. Combining it with strategies like self-consistency can help address some of these limitations. These observations were presented in Self-consistency Improves Chain of Thought Reasoning in Language Models[38] (Wang, X., Wei, J., Schuurmans, D., Le, Q., Chi, E., Narang, S., Chowdhery, A., & Zhou, D. (2022)).

Self-consistency is a strategy to enhance the model's reasoning abilities.

Back to the metaphor we used, our hiker stands at the crossroads of several trails, each claiming to lead to the most scenic spot in the forest. Instead of choosing one at random, the hiker consults different maps, asks other experimented hikers, and even observes where the majority seem to be headed. If all these sources point to the same trail, the hiker would feel confident in choosing that path. This verification from multiple sources shows the idea of self-consistency in reasoning and decision-making.

Similarly, if you're trying to solve a math problem, instead of just using one method to find the answer, you use several different methods. If all these methods lead to the same answer, you'd be pretty confident that your answer is correct. That's the simplified main idea behind self-consistency.

In technical terms, when a language model is given a problem, instead of just rushing to the most obvious answer, it explores multiple reasoning paths. Each path might suggest a different answer. The model then checks which answer

---

[38]https://arxiv.org/pdf/2203.11171.pdf

appears most consistently across these paths. Just as humans have different ways of thinking and approaching problems, this diversity can be simulated in language models.

The idea is that the more often an answer appears, the more likely it is to be correct. Here's how it works:

- Prompt the model: Start by giving the model a question and some examples of how to reason through it.
- Generate multiple answers: Instead of just getting one answer, let the model think of several possible reasoning paths.
- Pick the most consistent answer: From the multiple answers the model comes up with, choose the one that appears most frequently.

When the model thinks of multiple solutions, it's like sampling different paths of reasoning. These paths are then weighed based on their likelihood. The final answer is chosen based on which answer appears most frequently among these paths.

When compared to other methods, self-consistency "consistently" performed better. Even in situations where adding a step-by-step reasoning process might not be beneficial, self-consistency still improved performance. In addition, it proved to be better than other popular techniques like beam search[39] and ensemble-based approaches[40].

The technique was tested on various tasks and models, and the results were impressive. When combined with certain models like PaLM-540B or GPT-3, self-consistency set new performance records on several reasoning tasks. For instance, on the GSM8K task, there was an improvement of 17.9% in accuracy.

In practice, if we take this questions:

```
If you have 5 apples and eat 2, how many are left?
```

The model using CoT might use the following reasoning path as a learning example:

---

[39]https://en.wikipedia.org/wiki/Beam_search
[40]https://en.wikipedia.org/wiki/Ensemble_learning

```
You start with 5 apples. You eat 2 of them. So, 5 minus 2 equals 3 appl\
es. The answer is 3 apples left.
```

On the other hand, self-consistency models explores multiple ways of thinking about a problem to ensure its answer is correct. For the same question, the model might be prompted to think of different ways to solve it, such as:

```
You had 5 apples and after eating 2, you have 3 left
```

and

```
Start with 5 apples, and if 2 are gone when eaten, that leaves 3 apples
```

and

```
If there were 5 apples and 2 are no longer there because you ate them, \
then 5 minus 2 equals 3 apples remaining.
```

Since all these different reasoning paths lead to the answer "3 apples", the model gains confidence that 3 is the correct answer. So, while CoT provides a clear breakdown of the thought process, self-consistency cross-checks the problem in various ways to ensure the reliability of the answer.

When implementing self-consistency, it's recommended to provide as many examples as possible. This helps the model explore more reasoning paths and increases the chances of finding the correct answer. This file named "test_socratic.jsonl[41]" on OpenAI GitHub repository is a good example.

Let's ask OpenAI text-davinci-002 the following question:

```
If there are 3 cars in the parking lot and 2 more cars arrive, 1 car le\
aves, 15 cars arrives and 8 leaves, how many cars are in the parking?"
```

This is the Python code:

---

[41]https://github.com/openai/grade-school-math/blob/master/grade_school_math/data/test_socratic.jsonl

```
import openai
import os

openai.api_key = os.getenv("OPENAI_API_KEY")

prompt = """
Q: If there are 3 cars in the parking lot and 2 more cars arrive, 1 car\
 leaves, 15 cars arrives and 8 leaves, how many cars are in the parking
?"
A:
"""
# the answer should be: 3 + 2 - 1 + 15 - 8 = 11

response = openai.Completion.create(
  engine="text-davinci-002",
  prompt=prompt,
  temperature=0.5,
  max_tokens=260
)
print(response.choices[0].text.strip())
```

The answer is incorrect as it returned:

```
There are 18 cars in the parking lot.
```

To improve the answer, we can use the few-shot examples provided in the paper[42]:

---

[42]https://arxiv.org/abs/2203.11171

```python
import openai
import os

openai.api_key = os.getenv("OPENAI_API_KEY")

# Few shot learning to improve the accuracy of the model
prompt = """
Q: There are 15 trees in the grove. Grove workers will plant trees in t\
he grove today. After they are done,
there will be 21 trees. How many trees did the grove workers plant toda\
y?
A: We start with 15 trees. Later we have 21 trees. The difference must \
be the number of trees they planted.
So, they must have planted 21 - 15 = 6 trees. The answer is 6.
Q: If there are 3 cars in the parking lot and 2 more cars arrive, how m\
any cars are in the parking lot?
A: There are 3 cars in the parking lot already. 2 more arrive. Now ther\
e are 3 + 2 = 5 cars. The answer is 5.
Q: Leah had 32 chocolates and her sister had 42. If they ate 35, how ma\
ny pieces do they have left in total?
A: Leah had 32 chocolates and Leah's sister had 42. That means there we\
re originally 32 + 42 = 74
chocolates. 35 have been eaten. So in total they still have 74 - 35 = 3\
9 chocolates. The answer is 39.
Q: Jason had 20 lollipops. He gave Denny some lollipops. Now Jason has \
12 lollipops. How many lollipops
did Jason give to Denny?
A: Jason had 20 lollipops. Since he only has 12 now, he must have given\
 the rest to Denny. The number of
lollipops he has given to Denny must have been 20 - 12 = 8 lollipops. T\
he answer is 8.
Q: Shawn has five toys. For Christmas, he got two toys each from his mo\
m and dad. How many toys does
he have now?
A: He has 5 toys. He got 2 from mom, so after that he has 5 + 2 = 7 toy\
s. Then he got 2 more from dad, so
```

in total he has 7 + 2 = 9 toys. The answer is 9.

Q: There were nine computers in the server room. Five more computers we\
re installed each day, from
monday to thursday. How many computers are now in the server room?

A: There are 4 days from monday to thursday. 5 computers were added eac\
h day. That means in total 4 * 5 =
20 computers were added. There were 9 computers in the beginning, so no\
w there are 9 + 20 = 29 computers.
The answer is 29.

Q: Michael had 58 golf balls. On tuesday, he lost 23 golf balls. On wed\
nesday, he lost 2 more. How many
golf balls did he have at the end of wednesday?

A: Michael initially had 58 balls. He lost 23 on Tuesday, so after that\
 he has 58 - 23 = 35 balls. On
Wednesday he lost 2 more so now he has 35 - 2 = 33 balls. The answer is\
 33.

Q: Olivia has $23. She bought five bagels for $3 each. How much money d\
oes she have left?

A: She bought 5 bagels for $3 each. This means she spent 5

Q: If there are 3 cars in the parking lot and 2 more cars arrive, 1 car\
 leaves, 15 cars arrives and 8 leaves, how many cars are in the parking
?"

A:
"""

the answer should be: 3 + 2 - 1 + 15 - 8 = 11

```python
response = openai.Completion.create(
    engine="text-davinci-002",
    prompt=prompt,
    temperature=0.5,
    max_tokens=260
)
print(response.choices[0].text.strip())
```

The answer is now correct:

There are 3 cars in the parking lot already. 2 more arrive. Now there a\
re 3 + 2 = 5 cars. 1 car leaves. So now there are 5 - 1 = 4 cars. 15 mo
re cars arrive. So now there are 4 + 15 = 19 cars. 8 cars leave. So now
 there are 19 - 8 = 11 cars. The answer is 11.

11: Transfer Learning

11.1: What is transfer learning?

Transfer learning (TL), by definition, is the improvement of learning in a new task through the transfer of knowledge from a related task that has already been learned. The related task is typically either a task from the same domain or a task from a different domain that has shared concepts or shared low-level features.

The idea of transfer learning is not new. In fact, it has been studied in the field of psychology and behaviorism for over 100 years. It was also used in pedagogy to teach children how to acquire new skills by building on what they already know.

These are some examples of transfer learning in the real world:

- If someone learned to play the piano, they might find it easier to learn another keyboard instrument like the organ, due to the similarities between the two instruments.
- A child who's learned to be wary of a hot stove might also avoid touching a barbecue grill without being explicitly taught.
- A child who learned to ride a tricycle might find it easier to learn to ride a bicycle than a child who has never ridden a tricycle.

TL has only recently become a popular topic in the field of machine learning.

For example, when applied in image classification, transfer learning can be used to reuse knowledge gained while solving a problem in one domain (e.g., recognizing reptiles) to solve a problem in another domain (e.g., recognizing amphibians).

In other words, TL is reusing a pre-trained model as a starting point for a new task. In the context of LLMs, this method allows us to leverage knowledge learned from huge datasets and apply it to a specific problem. There are two main approaches to transfer learning: inductive transfer and transductive transfer. Both approaches are based on the idea that knowledge learned in one task can be used to improve performance in another task.

Let's take a look at each approach in more detail.

11.2: Inductive transfer

Inductive transfer is a prevalent approach in transfer learning. It's about the ability of a learning mechanism to leverage knowledge or skills from one task to improve performance on another related, but distinct, task.

In simple terms, inductive transfer occurs when a system becomes more proficient at a current task due to its previous experiences with similar tasks. It's analogous to applying previously learned knowledge or a specific way of thinking to new challenges.

Consider language acquisition as an example. If you first learn Spanish and later decide to pick up Portuguese, your proficiency in Spanish aids your learning process because of the many similarities between the two languages. This exemplifies inductive transfer: the knowledge of Spanish bolsters the learning of Portuguese.

Similarly, in machine learning, a model that has been trained to recognize English handwriting might find it easier to identify handwritten letters in related languages such as French, Italian, Spanish, or Portuguese.

11.3: Transductive transfer

Transductive transfer, in contrast to inductive transfer, focuses on leveraging knowledge from specific instances in one domain to make predictions on specific instances in a closely related domain, all while the underlying task remains constant.

Take, for instance, a student adept at solving math problems in class using methods they've encountered in their textbook. When faced with a slightly varied problem in an exam, they might recall a textbook problem and replicate its solution method, bypassing a true understanding of the underlying mathematical principle.

To draw a parallel in machine learning, specifically in the field of computer vision, imagine a system trained to distinguish between cats and dogs in photos from a particular shelter. When presented with images from an unfamiliar shelter, using transductive transfer, the system would attempt to categorize these new images based on the specific examples it encountered from the original shelter, rather than generalizing the broader notion of distinguishing between cats and dogs in varied environments.

11.4: Inductive vs. transductive transfer

Inductive and transductive learning methodologies can sometimes appear similar, but a closer look reveals that there are distinct differences in their approaches.

In inductive learning, the model is trained using only a set of labeled data and then seeks to generalize, predicting labels for data it hasn't seen. This general model can be readily applied to any new data within the same domain.

Conversely, transductive learning directly encounters both the labeled training and unlabeled testing data during its training process. Unlike induction, it doesn't aim to create a generalized model; instead, it focuses on predicting the labels of the specific unlabeled data it has seen, based on its knowledge of the labeled data and other relevant information. This specificity means that introducing new data often requires the algorithm to start afresh – a process that can be both time-consuming and computationally expensive, especially with streaming data.

While inductive learning emphasizes broad applicability, transductive learning optimizes for the data at hand. Knowing when to use each approach can be instrumental in various machine learning applications.

In simpler words, inductive learning reasoning progresses from observed training cases and seeks to generalize to unseen scenarios while transductive learning reasoning moves from specific observed cases to other specific yet unseen cases, without altering the fundamental task at hand.

To draw a parallel from psychology, "Hugging", suggested by Perkins and Salomon (1989)[43], which emphasizes the similarities between the learning situation and

---

[43]https://jaymctighe.com/wp-content/uploads/2011/04/Transfer-of-Learning-Perkins-and-Salomon.pdf

future applications, can be likened to inductive learning, while "Bridging" another technique used in teaching, which connects specific instances of knowledge to new situations, mirrors the principles of transductive learning.

This table summarizes the differences between inductive and transductive learning:

Aspect	Inductive Learning	Transductive Learning
Encountered Data	Only encounters training data during model training.	Encounters both training and testing datasets during model training.
Predictive Model	Builds a predictive model that can be applied to unseen data.	Does not construct a standalone predictive model for unseen data.
New Data Handling	When new data is introduced, the established model can quickly predict without retraining.	New data necessitates rerunning the algorithm from the start, retraining, and then predicting.
Model's Purpose	Seeks to create a general model capable of predicting any new point within the data space.	Constructs a model tailored to the specific training and testing data points it has encountered.
Efficiency with Streams	Can rapidly label new data points with minimal computational overhead.	Can become computationally intensive if new data points are continuously introduced.

11.5: Transfer learning, fine-tuning, and prompt engineering

Prompt engineering and transfer learning serve different purposes but are both methodologies used to improve the performance and utility of machine learning models, particularly in the context of models like OpenAI's GPT series.

Fine-tuning is a type of transfer learning that involves taking a pre-trained model and adapting it to a new custom task. It's a common practice in the field of natural language processing (NLP) and is often used to improve the performance of language models.

But what's the relationship between prompt engineering and fine-tuning?

When you want to fine-tune a model like OpenAI GPT, you need to provide it with a set of training examples that each consist of a single input ("prompt") and its associated output ("completion"). This is notably different from using the base models, where you might input detailed instructions or multiple examples in a single prompt.

This is useful when you want to the model to perform a specific task. For example, you might want to fine-tune a model to understand your customer support tickets and respond to them automatically based on the your knowledge base or previous responses to similar tickets.

11.6: Fine-tuning with a prompt dataset: a practical example

For the sake of simplicity, we are going to use one of OpenAI base models and fine-tune it to perform a simple task: answer questions about from a FAQ.

To fine-tune a model, we will need a set of training examples that each consist of a single input ("prompt") and its associated output ("completion") as described previously. Here is what OpenAI documentation recommends:

- Each prompt should end with a fixed separator to inform the model when the prompt ends and the completion begins. A simple separator which generally works well is \n\n###\n\n. The separator should not appear elsewhere in any prompt.

- Each completion should start with a whitespace due to their (OpenAI) tokenization, which tokenizes most words with a preceding whitespace.
- Each completion should end with a fixed stop sequence to inform the model when the completion ends. A stop sequence could be \n, ###, or any other token that does not appear in any completion.

Say you have an e-learning platform called SkillUp Academy, and you also have the following FAQ page.

```
Q. What is SkillUp Academy?
A. SkillUp Academy is an online learning platform offering a variety of\
 courses across multiple disciplines, enabling learners to gain knowled
ge and skills at their own pace from anywhere in the world.

Q. How do I sign up?
A. Just click on the "Sign Up" button on our homepage, provide your det\
ails, and get started!

Q. How can I pay for a course?
A. We accept payments through PayPal, and Stripe.

Q. I am not satisfied with the course. Can I get a refund?
A. Yes, we offer a 30-day money-back guarantee. If you're not satisfied\
 within this period, you can request a refund. Please see our refund po
licy for details.

Q. Where can I find the terms of service for the website?
A. Our terms of service can be found at the footer of our website or by\
 clicking here.

Q. Is my personal information secure?
A. Absolutely. We prioritize your privacy and have stringent measures i\
n place to protect your data. Read more in our privacy policy here.
```

Q. Can I learn at my own pace?
A. Yes, our courses are designed to allow you to learn at your convenie\
nce. Once you enroll, you'll have access to the course materials for a
specific period, during which you can learn at your own pace.

Q. I have questions about the course content. How can I get them answer\
ed?
A. Most courses have a discussion forum where you can ask questions, en\
gage with fellow learners, and sometimes get responses from the course
instructors.

Q. Can I access the courses on mobile?
A. Yes, our platform is mobile-friendly, and we also have a dedicated a\
pp available for both Android and iOS.

Q. I'm an instructor. How can I offer a course on your platform?
A. We're always looking for knowledgeable instructors. Just head to our\
 'Become an Instructor' page for details on how to collaborate with us.

Q. Do you offer certificates upon course completion?
A. Yes, once you successfully complete a course and pass any required a\
ssessments, you will receive a certificate of completion.

Q. What should I do if I face technical issues?
A. Please reach out to our support team via the 'Contact Us' page, and \
they'll be happy to assist you.

In order to use the FAQ as a training dataset, we need to convert it into a format
that OpenAI GPT can understand. We will use a format that is similar to the one
recommended by OpenAI (JSONL document[44])

---

[44]https://jsonlines.org/

```
{"prompt": "lorem ipsum dolor sit amet.END_PROMPT", "completion": " con\
sectetur adipiscing elit.\n"}
{"prompt": "Vivamus vel lacus quis diam vestibulum scelerisque.END_PROM\
PT", "completion": " Pellentesque habitant morbi tristique senectus et
netus et malesuada fames ac turpis egestas.\n"}
...etc
```

In practice, the lorem ipsum texts will be replaced by the question (prompt) and the answer (completion). The -> and \n are the separators that we will use to inform the model when prompts and completions end.

This is how the FAQ dataset will look like:

```
{"prompt": "What is SkillUp Academy->", "completion": " SkillUp Academy\
 is an online learning platform offering a variety of courses across mu
ltiple disciplines, enabling learners to gain knowledge and skills at t
heir own pace from anywhere in the world.\n"}
{"prompt": "How do I sign up->", "completion": " Just click on the \"Si\
gn Up\" button on our homepage, provide your details, and get started!\
n"}
{"prompt": "How can I pay for a course->", "completion": " We accept pa\
yments through PayPal, and Stripe.\n"}
{"prompt": "I am not satisfied with the course. Can I get a refund->", \
"completion": " Yes, we offer a 30-day money-back guarantee. If you're
not satisfied within this period, you can request a refund. Please see
our refund policy for details.\n"}
{"prompt": "Where can I find the terms of service for the website->", "\
completion": " Our terms of service can be found at the footer of our w
ebsite or by clicking here.\n"}
{"prompt": "Is my personal information secure->", "completion": " Absol\
utely. We prioritize your privacy and have stringent measures in place
to protect your data. Read more in our privacy policy here.\n"}
{"prompt": "Can I learn at my own pace->", "completion": " Yes, our cou\
rses are designed to allow you to learn at your convenience. Once you e
nroll, you'll have access to the course materials for a specific period
, during which you can learn at your own pace.\n"}
```

```
{"prompt": "I have questions about the course content. How can I get th\
em answered->", "completion": " Most courses have a discussion forum wh
ere you can ask questions, engage with fellow learners, and sometimes g
et responses from the course instructors.\n"}
{"prompt": "Can I access the courses on mobile->", "completion": " Yes,\
 our platform is mobile-friendly, and we also have a dedicated app avai
lable for both Android and iOS.\n"}
{"prompt": "I'm an instructor. How can I offer a course on your platfor\
m->", "completion": " We're always looking for knowledgeable instructor
s. Just head to our 'Become an Instructor' page for details on how to c
ollaborate with us.\n"}
{"prompt": "Do you offer certificates upon course completion->", "compl\
etion": " Yes, once you successfully complete a course and pass any req
uired assessments, you will receive a certificate of completion.\n"}
{"prompt": "What should I do if I face technical issues->", "completion\
": " Please reach out to our support team via the 'Contact Us' page, an
d they'll be happy to assist you.\n"}
```

Note that we removed the "?" from the prompts.

Next, install the OpenAI command-line interface (CLI):

```
pip install openai[datalib]
```

Export your OpenAI API key:

```
export OPENAI_API_KEY=<your-api-key>
```

Save the JSONL file to data.jsonl and run the following command:

```
openai tools fine_tunes.prepare_data -f data.jsonl
```

You should be able to see a similar output:

```
Analyzing...

- Your file contains 12 prompt-completion pairs. In general, we recomme\
nd having at least a few hundred examples. We've found that performance
 tends to linearly increase for every doubling of the number of example
s
- All prompts end with suffix `->`
- All completions end with suffix `\n`

No remediations found.

You can use your file for fine-tuning:
> openai api fine_tunes.create -t "data.jsonl"

After you've fine-tuned a model, remember that your prompt has to end w\
ith the indicator string `->` for the model to start generating complet
ions, rather than continuing with the prompt. Make sure to include `sto
p=["\n"]` so that the generated texts ends at the expected place.
Once your model starts training, it'll approximately take 2.61 minutes \
to train a `curie` model, and less for `ada` and `babbage`. Queue will
approximately take half an hour per job ahead of you.
```

Now, we can fine-tune the model using the following command:

```
openai api fine_tunes.create -t "data.jsonl" -m curie --suffix "SkillUp\
Academy"
```

You should be able to see a similar output:

```
Upload progress: 100%|□□□□□□□□□□□□□□□□□□□□□□□□□□□□□□□□□□□□□□□□□□□□□□□□□□□\
□□□□□□□□□□□□□□□□□□□□□□□□□□□□□□□□□□□□□□□□□□□□□□□□□□□□□□□□□□□□□□□□□□□□□□□□□□□□□
□□□□□□□□□□□□□□□□□□□□□□□□□| 2.47k/2.47k [00:00<00:00, 8.63Mit/s]
Uploaded file from data.jsonl: file-RdACszHknKQC49hdZdGxpoEA
Created fine-tune: ft-WEYpsygNbeHy8YvxLCaiyB4i
Streaming events until fine-tuning is complete...

(Ctrl-C will interrupt the stream, but not cancel the fine-tune)
[..] Created fine-tune: ft-WEYpsygNbeHy8YvxLCaiyB4i
[..] Fine-tune costs $0.01
[..] Fine-tune enqueued. Queue number: 0

...etc
```

As said by the output, you can exit the stream by pressing `Ctrl-C`, this won't cancel the fine-tune job. You can also check the status of the fine-tune job by running the following command:

```
openai api fine_tunes.follow -i ft-WEYpsygNbeHy8YvxLCaiyB4i
```

Where `ft-WEYpsygNbeHy8YvxLCaiyB4i` is the fine-tune ID.

When the fine-tune job is completed, you will see a similar output to this one:

```
[..] Created fine-tune: ft-WEYpsygNbeHy8YvxLCaiyB4i
[..] Fine-tune costs $0.01
[..] Fine-tune enqueued. Queue number: 0
[..] Fine-tune started
[..] Completed epoch 1/4
[..] Completed epoch 2/4
[..] Completed epoch 3/4
[..] Completed epoch 4/4
[..] Uploaded model: curie:ft-org:skillupacademy-2023-08-18-14-32-18
[..] Uploaded result file: file-3fxL6gfapDyHqG7cjXDzFFOf
[..] Fine-tune succeeded
```

```
Job complete! Status: succeeded 🎉
Try out your fine-tuned model:
```

```
openai api completions.create -m curie:ft-faun:skillupacademy-2023-08-1\
8-14-32-18 -p <YOUR_PROMPT>
```

Let's try it out:

```python
import openai
import os

openai.api_key = os.getenv("OPENAI_API_KEY")

model = "curie:ft-faun:skillupacademy-2023-08-18-14-32-18"
prompt = input("Ask a question: ")
instruction = f"""
You are a helpful and smart customer service representative for SkillUp\
 Academy.
Answer the following questions based on the training data provided.
If you don't know the answer, just say 'Sorry, I don't know the answer.'

AI: Hi there. I am Felix, the chatbot. How can I help you today?
User: {prompt}
"""

full_prompt = instruction + " " + prompt + "->"

response = openai.Completion.create(
    model=model,
    prompt=full_prompt,
    max_tokens=100,   # adjust based on your need
    stop=["\n"],
    temperature=0   # strikes a balance between deterministic and random
)

print(response.choices[0].text.strip())
```

The training data is very limited, so the model will not be able to answer all the questions with 100% accuracy, however, it works well for a good number of questions.

The goal of this example is to show you how to fine-tune a model using a prompt dataset. In practice, you will need to use a larger dataset to get better results and use better, well-studied prompts.

11.7: Why is prompt engineering vital for transfer learning and fine-tuning?

Transfer learning, particularly in the context of large language models like GPT, refers to the application of knowledge gained while solving one problem to solve a different, but related, problem. In the context of OpenAI's GPT and fine-tuning, it essentially means taking the vast knowledge already encoded within the base GPT model and refining or redirecting it with a smaller, domain-specific dataset. This is what we see in the example above where GPT is fine-tuned with a specific dataset related to "SkillUp Academy."

However, merely possessing a fine-tuned model isn't the end of the story. The way we interface with that model—how we phrase our prompts—plays a crucial role in the kind of responses we receive. This is where the art and science of prompt engineering come into play.

Prompt engineering plays a central role in the success of fine-tuning for these 5 main reasons:

1 - Improving accuracy: Even with a perfectly fine-tuned model, imprecise or ambiguous prompts can lead to misleading or unhelpful answers. A well-engineered prompt helps guide the model towards the most relevant and accurate response.

2 - Exploiting model knowledge: Given the vast knowledge within GPT, a well-phrased prompt can extract nuanced information, even if the specific fine-tuning data did not cover it. It's like fine-tuning provides the specialization, while prompt engineering ensures we can still leverage the broader general knowledge of the base model.

3 - Guiding context: Especially in customer service or domain-specific applications, setting the right context is essential. For instance, in the given example, the instruction sets the model in a customer service role for SkillUp Academy. Without this context, the model might respond in a generic fashion, unaware of its specialized role.

4 - Handling unknowns gracefully: A good prompt can also instruct the model on how to handle questions it might not know, as seen with the "Sorry, I don't know the answer." instruction. This can be particularly useful in avoiding "hallucinations" or spurious answers.

5 - Maximizing efficiency: In some cases, you might be limited by token counts or computational constraints. A concise and clear prompt ensures that the model's computational power is directed towards generating valuable output, rather than deciphering a vague question.

On the other hand, while prompt engineering has its advantages, it also comes with challenges:

- Iterative process: Finding the perfect prompt often requires multiple iterations and testing.
- Overfitting: Over-optimizing a prompt for specific questions might lead to reduced performance on broader or slightly different questions.
- Training data limitations: No matter how expertly crafted the prompt, if the fine-tuning data is sparse or of low quality, the model's responses will be limited in accuracy and relevance.

In this fine-tuning example, GPT provides a powerful mechanism to specialize the model for a particular domain (client support). Still, prompt engineering is the bridge between this specialized knowledge and the user's questions. Like any tool, the quality of the output depends not just on the tool's capability, but also on the expertise of the user.

As LLMs continue to grow and become more integrated into more industries and applications, prompt engineering will emerge as a key skill in fine-tuning and transfer learning.

12: Perplexity as a metric for prompt optimization

12.1: Do not surprise the model

Language models, when given prompts, could tackle a wide array of tasks with little to no prior examples. However, their effectiveness hinged greatly on the selected prompt. The reasons for this variation weren't entirely clear. Some researchers dived into the factors causing this discrepancy and proposed an idea: the better the model recognized the language in the prompt, the more effectively it performed. Essentially, prompts that were more familiar or "natural" to the model yielded better outcomes.

In simpler terms, prompts that are more common in the training data tend to perform better. This is because familiar sequences help the model understand and provide relevant information. However, it's challenging to gauge this precisely since many language models are trained on vast data, and we don't always have access to this data, like in the case of OpenAI GPT models.

This hypothesis was studied in the paper "Demystifying Prompts in Language Models via Perplexity Estimation[45]" (Gonen, H., Iyer, S., Blevins, T., Smith, N. A., & Zettlemoyer, L. (2022)). We are not going to dive deep into the details of the paper but the authors stated that over a wide range of tasks, the lower the perplexity of the prompt (i.e. closer to zero) is, the better the prompt is able to perform the task.

Instead of considering the training data, the paper proposes perplexity of the prompt as a proxy used to gauge how often it might appear in the data. This method helps bypass the issue of finding an exact match and considers similar versions of the prompt. It's also beneficial because we don't need to access the vast training data, which isn't always open to the public.

---

[45]https://arxiv.org/pdf/2212.04037.pdf

Over a wide range of tasks, we show that the lower the perplexity of the prompt is, the better the prompt is able to perform the task.

Perplexity is a measure or a metric of how well the model predicts a sample. A lower perplexity means the model is more certain and accurate in its predictions, while a higher perplexity indicates uncertainty. Think of perplexity as the model's level of "surprise". If a model reads a sentence and predicts the next word correctly without much doubt, it has low perplexity - it's not very "surprised" by the actual next word because it expected it. Conversely, if it struggles to predict the next word, its perplexity is high - it's more "surprised" by the actual word that comes next.

This of this like giving someone a task in a language they are fluent in versus a language they've just started learning. Naturally, they'd perform better with the familiar language.

12.2: How to calculate perplexity?

In general, perplexity is calculated using the following formula:

PP(s) = p(w1, w2, ..., wN)^(-1/N)

Where:

- **s** is the sample
- **wx** is word from the sample
- **N** is the number of words in the sample
- **p(wx)** is the probability of the word

If all words are independent, the formula can be simplified to:

p(w1, w2, ..., wN) = p(w1) * p(w2) * ... * p(wN)

In case, the next word depends only on the previous word, the formula can be simplified to:

p(w1,w2,w3,...,wN) = p(w1) * p(w2|w1) * p(w3|w2) * ... * p(wN|wN-1)

To implement the above formula directly, you'd need the joint probability of the entire sequence. However, models typically provide probabilities (or log probabilities) for one word at a time. That's why we often work with a modified formulas.

For a given word w with probability p(w), , its log probability is log(p(w)). If we're looking at the likelihood of a sequence, instead of multiplying the probabilities, we add the log probabilities: log(p(w1,w2,w3,...,wN)) = log(p(w1)) + log(p(w2)) + ... + log(p(wN))

However, for log probabilities, a 'good' or 'likely' event has a high log probability (close to 0), whereas an 'unlikely' event has a very negative log probability. We sometimes talk about the "negative log likelihood" (NLL), which is just the negative of the log probability. A higher NLL indicates a less likely event.

Given that we have the NLL for each word in a sequence, the average NLL is: avg NLL= -log(p(w1)) - log(p(w2)) - ... - log(p(wN)) / N The perplexity is then: PP = exp(avg NLL).

A practical example using an OpenAI language model translated to Python would be:

```python
import os
import openai
import math

# Set the model name.
model_name = "<MODEL_NAME>"

# Set the API key for OpenAI.
openai_api_key = os.environ["OPENAI_API_KEY"]
openai.api_key = openai_api_key

# Define the prompt you want to send to the model.
prompt = """
Once upon a time in a land far far away
"""
```

```python
# Send the prompt to the OpenAI API and get the response.
response = openai.Completion.create(
    model=model_name,
    prompt=prompt,
    max_tokens=0,
    echo=True,
    logprobs=0
)

# Extract the log probabilities from the response.
token_logprobs = response["choices"][0]["logprobs"]["token_logprobs"]

# Replace any None values with -100. The first word in the prompt will \
be None.
# The value -100 attributes a very low probability to the first word.
# By assigning a very low likelihood to the first word, we're saying we\
 have no confidence in the model's choice of that word as the start of
the sequence.
nlls = [-100 if x is None else x for x in token_logprobs]
perplexity = math.exp(sum(nlls) / len(token_logprobs))

# Print the perplexity.
print("Perplexity:", perplexity)
```

This code was inspired by Betterprompt and we are going to use it later in this chapter.

🛈 Perplexity applied to a text, could be used to detect if it was generated by a language model. If the perplexity is very low, it is likely that the text was generated by a language model. Some AI content detection tools, like GPTZero[46] use this technique to detect if a text was generated by ChatGPT.

---
[46]https://gptzero.me/

12.3: A practical example with Betterprompt

Betterprompt[47] is a test suite for LLM prompts before pushing them to production. This open source tools is inspired by the same paper, "Demystifying Prompts in Language Models via Perplexity Estimation[48]".

Betterprompt helps in calculating the perplexity of a prompt. If you want to test it, install the package:

```
pip install betterprompt
```

Run the following script:

```
import betterprompt
import os
prompt = input("Enter your prompt: ")
perplexity = betterprompt.calculate_perplexity(prompt)
print("Perplexity: " + str(perplexity))
```

Enter a prompt and the script will return the perplexity of the prompt. The lower the perplexity, the better the prompt is.

Let's test two similar prompts.

- **The first one is**: "Write a 100-word paragraph on the benefits of yoga for mental health. Focus on the calming effect of yoga on the nervous system, stress reduction, and improved concentration and mental clarity. Avoid talking about the physical aspects of yoga, and focus only on the aspects related to mental health."
- **The second one is**: "Compose a 100-word essay about how yoga positively impacts mental well-being. Highlight the calming influence on the mind, its role in reducing stress, and how it sharpens focus and clarity."

After executing the script, we get the following results:

---

[47]https://github.com/stjordanis/betterprompt
[48]https://arxiv.org/pdf/2212.04037.pdf

```
Perplexity: 0.01080151264470053
Perplexity: 0.004663176137461259
```

The second prompt has a lower perplexity, meaning it is more familiar to the model. Therefore, it should perform better. After testing both prompts with gpt-3.5-turbo, we get the following results:

- **First prompt result (higher perplexity):**

```
Yoga offers numerous benefits for mental health by nurturing a calm and\
 balanced state of mind. One of its key advantages lies in its ability
to soothe the nervous system, promoting deep relaxation and reducing st
ress levels. Through the practice of various breathing techniques and m
editation, yoga helps individuals achieve a sense of inner peace and tr
anquility. Additionally, regular yoga practice enhances concentration a
nd mental clarity, allowing individuals to better focus on their though
ts and emotions. By redirecting attention away from the external world
and towards the present moment, yoga acts as a powerful tool for improv
ing mental well-being and promoting overall mental health.
```

- **Second prompt result (lower perplexity):**

```
Yoga, with its centuries-old practice, has emerged as a powerful tool f\
or enhancing mental well-being. It exerts a calming influence on the mi
nd, inviting a sense of peace and serenity. Through controlled breathin
g and sustained postures, yoga reduces stress levels, allowing individu
als to better manage anxiety and overwhelm. Moreover, the practice prom
otes mindfulness and self-awareness, providing a much-needed respite fr
om the noise and distractions of the modern world. By cultivating focus
 and clarity, yoga sharpens cognitive abilities and improves decision-m
aking skills. Ultimately, yoga offers a holistic approach to mental wel
lness, fostering a sense of balance, tranquility, and improved overall
mental health.
```

There are no big differences between the two results but while the first text uses a more straightforward and instructive tone, the second text has a slightly more poetic and evocative tone, with phrases like "respite from the noise and distractions of the modern world."

Let's try two more prompts:

```
Enter your prompt: Generate a 2-day itinerary for a cultural trip to Ro\
me.
Perplexity: 8.967913713192179e-05

Enter your prompt: Craft a detailed 2-day cultural journey plan for vis\
iting Rome's historic landmarks and museums.
Perplexity: 3.844865699961805e-05
```

The second prompt has a lower perplexity, meaning it is more familiar to the model. After testing both prompts with gpt-3.5-turbo, we get the following results:

- **First prompt result (higher perplexity)**:

```
Certainly! Here's a suggested 2-day itinerary for a cultural trip to Ro\
me:

Day 1:
Morning:
1. Start your day by visiting the Colosseum, one of Rome's most iconic \
landmarks. Take a guided tour or explore it at your own pace.
2. After the Colosseum, head over to the Roman Forum, an ancient city c\
enter filled with ruins and historical sites. Spend some time exploring
 the area and learning about its significance in Roman history.
3. Visit the nearby Palatine Hill, which offers panoramic views of the \
city and is home to impressive archaeological remains.

Afternoon:
4. Enjoy a leisurely lunch at a local trattoria near the historic cente\
```

r.
5. After lunch, visit the Pantheon, a former Roman temple and now a rem\
arkable piece of architecture. Marvel at its magnificent dome and explo
re its interior.
6. Head to Piazza Navona, a vibrant square known for its beautiful baro\
que fountains. Take a stroll, admire the artworks, and perhaps grab a g
elato from one of the nearby gelaterias.

Evening:
7. Spend the evening exploring the charming neighborhood of Trastevere.\
 Wander through its narrow streets, visit its ancient churches, and ind
ulge in a delicious dinner at one of its cozy trattorias.
8. Wrap up your day with a visit to the Trevi Fountain. Throw a coin ov\
er your shoulder into the fountain to ensure your return to Rome in the
 future.

Day 2:
Morning:
1. Begin your day by visiting Vatican City, the smallest independent st\
ate in the world. Explore St. Peter's Basilica, the largest church in C
hristendom, and admire Michelangelo's masterpiece, the Sistine Chapel,
located in the Vatican Museums.
2. Take a walk through the Vatican Gardens, a tranquil oasis in the hea\
rt of the city.

Afternoon:
3. Enjoy lunch at one of the local restaurants near Vatican City.
4. Visit the Capitoline Museums, located on Capitoline Hill. These muse\
ums house an impressive collection of ancient Roman artifacts and artwo
rks, including the famous statue of Romulus and Remus.
5. Take a stroll through the picturesque streets of the Monti district,\
 known for its trendy boutiques, artisan shops, and charming cafes.

Evening:
6. As the sun sets, make your way to the Spanish Steps, a famous meetin\
g place in Rome. Climb to the top for panoramic views and soak up the l

ively atmosphere.
7. Indulge in a traditional Italian dinner at a restaurant in the trend\
y neighborhood of Campo de' Fiori.
8. End your evening with a leisurely walk along the Tiber River, enjoyi\
ng the beautiful views of Rome's illuminated bridges and monuments.

Please note that this itinerary can be customized based on your specifi\
c interests and preferences. Enjoy your cultural trip to Rome!

- **Second prompt result (lower perplexity)**:

Sure! Here's a detailed 2-day cultural journey plan for visiting Rome's\
 historic landmarks and museums:

Day 1:
Morning:
1. Start your day by visiting the Colosseum, a magnificent amphitheater\
 that is a symbol of ancient Rome. Explore the interior and imagine the
 gladiator battles that once took place there.

2. Next, head to the Roman Forum, located right next to the Colosseum. \
This was the social, political, and commercial center of ancient Rome.
Take a guided tour or explore the area on your own to see the ancient r
uins and learn about its rich history.

3. Afterward, visit the Palatine Hill, which offers stunning views of t\
he city. This is where Romulus founded Rome and where many emperors bui
lt their palaces. Explore the archaeological site and the beautiful gar
dens.

Afternoon:
4. Take a short walk to the Capitoline Museums, located on Capitoline H\
ill. Here, you can admire a vast collection of sculptures, paintings, a
nd ancient Roman artifacts. Don't miss the famous statue of Marcus Aure
lius on horseback.

5. Enjoy a leisurely lunch in the charming neighborhood of Trastevere. \
This area is known for its narrow cobblestone streets, colorful buildin
gs, and delicious local cuisine.

6. In the afternoon, visit the Pantheon, one of the best-preserved anci\
ent Roman buildings. Marvel at its impressive dome and explore the inte
rior, which houses the tombs of several notable figures, including Raph
ael.

Evening:
7. Spend the evening at Piazza Navona, a lively square surrounded by be\
autiful Baroque buildings. Admire the Fountain of the Four Rivers and t
he stunning architecture. Enjoy dinner at one of the many restaurants i
n the area and savor the vibrant atmosphere.

Day 2:
Morning:
1. Start your second day by visiting the Vatican City, home to some of \
the world's most renowned museums and St. Peter's Basilica. Begin with
the Vatican Museums and immerse yourself in the vast collection of art,
 including the Sistine Chapel with its iconic ceiling painted by Michel
angelo.

2. Continue to St. Peter's Basilica, the largest church in the world. E\
xplore the stunning interior, marvel at Michelangelo's Pieta, and consi
der climbing to the top of the dome for a panoramic view of the city.

Afternoon:
3. After lunch, head to the Borghese Gallery, housed in the beautiful V\
illa Borghese. This museum features an impressive collection of sculptu
res and paintings by masters such as Bernini and Caravaggio. Reserve yo
ur tickets in advance as entry is timed.

4. Take a leisurely stroll through the charming neighborhood of Piazza \
di Spagna (Spanish Steps). Admire the famous Spanish Steps and explore

```
the nearby high-end shops and boutiques.

Evening:
5. End your cultural journey with a visit to the Trevi Fountain. Toss a\
 coin into the fountain for good luck before enjoying a traditional Ita
lian dinner at one of the local trattorias in the area.

Remember to wear comfortable shoes, carry a map or use a navigation app\
, and allow for some flexibility in your itinerary in case you want to
spend more time at any particular location. Enjoy your trip to Rome!
```

I asked ChatGPT to compare both itineraries and here its conclusion:

```
While both responses are excellent and would serve a traveler very well\
, the second itinerary edges out slightly due to its richer description
s, practical advice, and smoother transitions. It paints a slightly mor
e vivid picture of what the experience might be like. However, personal
 preference will play a significant role; some might prefer the simplic
ity and directness of the first itinerary.
```

Even if we can not take this conclusion as a reference, it seems that the second prompt, with a lower perplexity, is more familiar to the model and performs better.

12.4: Hack the prompt

With a lower perplexity, the prompt is more familiar to the model and performs better. But how can we lower the perplexity of a prompt?

What if we ask the model to create the prompt for us? This technique could be useful since the model is more familiar with the language it generates according to what we learned in the previous section.

Imagine you want to ask the model the following question:

```
Write a blog post about aging gracefully.
```

We can use the following prompt to ask the model to create a prompt for us:

```
Write a list of prompts that I will use to write a blog post about agin\
g gracefully.
```

If you already have a list of prompts, you can ask the model to paraphrase them for you.

```
Paraphrase the following prompts:
1. What does aging gracefully mean to you personally?
2. Why is the topic of aging gracefully so important in today's society?
...
```

13: ReAct: Reason + Act

13.1: What is it?

The ReAct (Reason + Act) framework represents an approach in the field of Large Language Models.

Think of ReAct like a chef who not only tells you the recipe step-by-step but also occasionally steps out to get fresh ingredients.

In this case, the "reasoning" part of ReAct is like the chef explaining each step. It allows the model to formulate plans, adjust them when necessary, and tackle unexpected issues.

The "act" part is when our chef fetches the ingredients. This represents the model's ability to communicate with external databases or tools to gather new data or insights, ensuring its responses are accurate and up-to-date. When ReAct combines these two capabilities, reasoning and acting, it does so in a coordinated manner, much like a chef adjusting a recipe based on the ingredients available.

This innovative blend allows ReAct to perform exceptionally well on tasks, producing solutions that are both human-like and easily understood, ultimately boosting our confidence in the model's abilities.

In a research paper titled ReAct: Synergizing Reasoning and Acting in Language Models.[49] (Yao, S., Zhao, J., Yu, D., Du, N., Shafran, I., Narasimhan, K., & Cao, Y. (2022)), the authors studied how Large Language Models can be made more effective by combining reasoning (like thinking through steps) and acting (like making plans). Instead of studying them separately, they interweave the two.

> Language models are getting better at reasoning (e.g. chain-of-thought prompting) and acting (e.g. WebGPT, SayCan, ACT-1), but these two directions have remained separate.

---

[49] https://arxiv.org/pdf/2210.03629.pdf

This means the model can think through its steps, adjust its plans, and even gather more data from outside sources. They named this approach "ReAct." They tested ReAct on various tasks, like answering questions and verifying facts, and it performed very well. For example, when tasked with answering questions or verifying facts, ReAct could avoid common mistakes by using a Wikipedia API. It also did better than other methods on tasks like online shopping, showing its effectiveness and adaptability in different situations.

> On two interactive decision making benchmarks (ALFWorld and WebShop), ReAct outperforms imitation and reinforcement learning methods by an absolute success rate of 34% and 10% respectively, while being prompted with only one or two in-context examples.

We are going to better understand ReAct by looking at a practical example.

13.2: ReAct using LanChain

Let's say we want to ask the model the following questions:

```
# Question 1
Roden Cutler House is owned by an electricity infrastructure company th\
at is owned by the Government of New South Wales, Australia, and was fo
rmed in what year?


# Question 2
Who was born first, Alan Paton or Jaroslav Seifert?


# Question 3
Anna Popplewell played Lady Lola in a series that follows what ?
```

These questions were randomly picked from hotpotqa.github.io[50] dataset.

To incorporate additional information into the reasoning, we are going to use the Wikipedia Python library to fetch useful information. We are also going to use LangChain with OpenAI as an LLM.

---

[50]https://hotpotqa.github.io/

ℹ️ If you are not familiar with prompting using LangChain, there is a chapter in this guide that explains it in detail. In this case, we recommend you come back to this example after reading that chapter.

```python
from langchain import OpenAI, Wikipedia
from langchain.agents import initialize_agent, Tool
from langchain.agents import AgentType
from langchain.agents.react.base import DocstoreExplorer

# Wikipedia is the docstore that the agent will use to answer questions
docstore=DocstoreExplorer(Wikipedia())

# Tools are the functions that the agent can use to answer questions
tools = [
    Tool(
        name="Search",
        func=docstore.search,
        description="useful for when you need to ask with search"
    ),
    Tool(
        name="Lookup",
        func=docstore.lookup,
        description="useful for when you need to ask with lookup"
    )
]

# Define the agent that will be used to answer questions
llm = OpenAI(temperature=0, model_name="text-davinci-002")

# Initialize the agent
react = initialize_agent(
    tools, # List of tools this agent has access to.
    llm, # Language model to use as the agent.
    agent=AgentType.REACT_DOCSTORE, # Agent type to use. If None and ag\
ent_path is also None, will default to AgentType.ZERO_SHOT_REACT_DESCRI
PTION.
```

```
    verbose=True # Print out the agent's actions
    )

question = input("Ask a question: ")
react.run(question)
```

Now, let's see the agent in action with the first question: "Roden Cutler House is owned by an electricity infrastructure company that is owned by the Government of New South Wales, Australia, and was formed in what year?"

ReAct using LanChain

The agent first searches for "Roden Cutler House" and finds that it is owned by Ausgrid. It then searches for "Ausgrid" and finds that it was formed in 2011. It then uses this information to answer the question.

This is the text generated by the agent:

```
> Entering new AgentExecutor chain...
Thought: I need to search Roden Cutler House, find the electricity infr\
astructure company that owns it, then find the year it was formed.
Action: Search[Roden Cutler House]
Observation: Roden Cutler House is a skyscraper in Sydney, New South Wa\
les, Australia. It consists of 19 floors primarily office/commercial sp\
ace. Construction finished in 1975 and it is located at 24 Campbell Str\
eet, Sydney. The Antenna height is 112m and the structure height is 108\
m. The building is owned by Ausgrid and the lower floors house the City\
 South substation.
The building is named after Sir Roden Cutler, the longest-serving Gover\
nor of New South Wales and a Victoria Cross recipient. Roden Cutler won
```

the Victoria Cross in the 1941 Syrian campaign where he was wounded, r
equiring the amputation of a leg.[1]
Thought: Roden Cutler House is owned by Ausgrid. I need to find the yea\
r it was formed.
Action: Search[Ausgrid]
Observation: Ausgrid is an electricity distribution company which owns,\
 maintains and operates the electrical networks supplying 1.8 million c
ustomers servicing more than 4 million people in Sydney, the Central Co
ast and Hunter regions of New South Wales, Australia. It was formed in
2011 from the previously state-owned energy retailer/distributor, Energ
yAustralia, when the retail division of the company, along with the Ene
rgyAustralia brand, was sold by the Government of New South Wales, and
the remainder renamed Ausgrid.
Thought: Ausgrid was formed in 2011. So the answer is 2011.
Action: Finish[2011]

> Finished chain.

Let's test with the second question: "Who was born first, Alan Paton or Jaroslav Seifert?"

```
> Entering new AgentExecutor chain...
Thought: I need to search Alan Paton and Jaroslav Seifert, and find who was born first.
Action: Search[Alan Paton]
Observation: Could not find [Alan Paton]. Similar: ['Alan Paton', 'David Paton', 'Sunday Times CNA Literary Awards', 'Lost in the Stars', 'The Alan Parsons Project',
'Deaths in 1988', 'Cry, the Beloved Country', 'Jonny Steinberg', 'Fred Khumalo', 'Liberalism in South Africa']
Thought: Alan Paton was born on January 11, 1903. I need to search Jaroslav Seifert next and find its date of birth.
Action: Search[Jaroslav Seifert]
Observation: Jaroslav Seifert (Czech: ['jaroslaf 'sajfrt] (listen); 23 September 1901 – 10 January 1986) was a Czech writer, poet and journalist. Seifert was awarded
the 1984 Nobel Prize in Literature "for his poetry which endowed with freshness, sensuality and rich inventiveness provides a liberating image of the indomitable spir
it and versatility of man".
Thought: Jaroslav Seifert was born on September 23, 1901. 1903 (Alan Paton) < 1901 (Jaroslav Seifert), so Jaroslav Seifert was born first.
Action: Finish[Jaroslav Seifert]
> Finished chain.
```

ReAct using LanChain

This is the text generated by the agent:

```
> Entering new AgentExecutor chain...
Thought: I need to search Alan Paton and Jaroslav Seifert, and find who\
 was born first.
Action: Search[Alan Paton]
Observation: Could not find [Alan Paton]. Similar: ['Alan Paton', 'Davi\
d Paton', 'Sunday Times CNA Literary Awards', 'Lost in the Stars', 'The
 Alan Parsons Project', 'Deaths in 1988', 'Cry, the Beloved Country', '
Jonny Steinberg', 'Fred Khumalo', 'Liberalism in South Africa']
Thought: Alan Paton was born on January 11, 1903. I need to search Jaro\
slav Seifert next and find its date of birth.
Action: Search[Jaroslav Seifert]
Observation: Jaroslav Seifert (Czech: [Ɋjaroslaf Ɋsajfr̩t] (listen); 23\
 September 1901 - 10 January 1986) was a Czech writer, poet and journal
ist. Seifert was awarded the 1984 Nobel Prize in Literature "for his po
etry which endowed with freshness, sensuality and rich inventiveness pr
ovides a liberating image of the indomitable spirit and versatility of
man".
Thought: Jaroslav Seifert was born on September 23, 1901. 1903 (Alan Pa\
ton) < 1901 (Jaroslav Seifert), so Jaroslav Seifert was born first.
Action: Finish[Jaroslav Seifert]

> Finished chain.
```

Finally, let's test with the third question: "Anna Popplewell played Lady Lola in a series that follows what?"

```
> Entering new AgentExecutor chain...
Thought: I need to search Anna Popplewell, find the series she played Lady Lola in, then find what the series follows.
Action: Search[Anna Popplewell]
Observation: Anna Katherine Popplewell (born 16 December 1988) is an English actress. Popplewell is known for playing Susan Pevensie in the fantasy film series The Ch
ronicles of Narnia (2005-2010), that earned her a number of accolades.
Aside from her The Chronicles of Narnia role, Popplewell played the role of Chyler Silva in the web series Halo 4: Forward Unto Dawn (2012) which is based on the vide
o game of the same name, and starred as Lady Lola in the historical romantic drama series Reign (2013-2016), which was her first leading role in a television series.
Thought: Anna Popplewell played Lady Lola in the historical romantic drama series Reign (2013-2016). So the series follows a historical romantic drama.
Action: Finish[historical romantic drama]

> Finished chain.
```

ReAct using LanChain

This is the text generated by the agent:

```
> Entering new AgentExecutor chain...
Thought: I need to search Anna Popplewell, find the series she played L\
ady Lola in, then find what the series follows.
Action: Search[Anna Popplewell]
Observation: Anna Katherine Popplewell (born 16 December 1988) is an En\
glish actress. Popplewell is known for playing Susan Pevensie in the fa
ntasy film series The Chronicles of Narnia (2005-2010), that earned her
 a number of accolades.
Aside from her The Chronicles of Narnia role, Popplewell played the rol\
e of Chyler Silva in the web series Halo 4: Forward Unto Dawn (2012) wh
ich is based on the video game of the same name, and starred as Lady Lo
la in the historical romantic drama series Reign (2013-2016), which was
 her first leading role in a television series.
Thought: Anna Popplewell played Lady Lola in the historical romantic dr\
ama series Reign (2013-2016). So the series follows a historical romant
ic drama.
Action: Finish[historical romantic drama]

> Finished chain.
```

As you can see from the execution logs, the agent was able to answer the questions correctly. It did this by using the Wikipedia API to find information about the topics in the questions. It then used this information to answer the questions.

14: General Knowledge Prompting

14.1: What is general knowledge prompting?

This was one of the most useful techniques I learned by testing and experimenting with ChatGPT first, before using it in production. It's a simple technique that can be used to improve the quality of the generated outputs.

In the paper Generated Knowledge Prompting for Commonsense Reasoning[51] (Liu, J., Liu, A., Lu, X., Welleck, S., West, P., Bras, R. L., Choi, Y., & Hajishirzi, H. (2021)), the authors tried to figure out if adding outside information helps in understanding common sense better while using trained language models. To test this, they created a method where they first generated knowledge from a model and then use that knowledge to answer questions. This method doesn't need special training or a database. It improved performance in several tasks and showed that big language models can be flexible sources of extra information.

The method uses two main steps to do this.

1. Knowledge generation: They used a language model to produce "knowledge statements" based on the given question. Think of these statements as pieces of information that can help answer the question.
2. Knowledge integration: They then used these knowledge statements to help another language model pick the best answer from the choices. Without these statements, the model would just try to guess the answer based only on the question.

---

[51]https://arxiv.org/pdf/2110.08387.pdf

14.2: Example of general knowledge prompting

This is an example of some prompts applying this technique. Let's say you want to ask the model the following question:

```
Write a short article about the advantages of using a chatbot on a webs\
ite.
```

We start by generating some knowledge statements that can help the model answer the question.

We can do this by generating knowledge statements from a model using these prompts:

```
What are the different types of chatbots? AI chatbots, rule-based chatb\
ots, live chat agents..etc
Why is it a good idea to use an AI chatbot on a website?
What are the benefits of using a AI chatbot?
Describe briefly the technical implementation process of an AI chatbot \
using OpenAI's API.
```

The generated knowledge will be used in the final prompt to help the model generate an article about the implementation of a smart chatbot on a website.

```
import os
import openai
openai.api_key = os.getenv("OPENAI_API_KEY")

print("=== Knowledge Generation 1 ===")
prompt1 = """
What are the different types of chatbots? AI chatbots, rule-based chatb\
ots, live chat agents..etc
"""

response1 = openai.Completion.create(
```

```python
    model="text-davinci-003",
    prompt=prompt1,
    temperature=1,
    max_tokens=500,
    top_p=1,
    frequency_penalty=0,
    presence_penalty=0
)
text1 = response1['choices'][0]['text']
print(text1)


print("=== Knowledge Generation 2 ===")
prompt2 = """
Why is it a good idea to use an AI chatbot on a website?
"""
response2 = openai.Completion.create(
    model="text-davinci-003",
    prompt=prompt2,
    temperature=1,
    max_tokens=500,
    top_p=1,
    frequency_penalty=0,
    presence_penalty=0
)
text2 = response2['choices'][0]['text']
print(text2)

print("=== Knowledge Generation 3 ===")
prompt3 = """
What are the benefits of using a AI chatbot?
"""
response3 = openai.Completion.create(
    model="text-davinci-003",
    prompt=prompt3,
    temperature=1,
```

```
    max_tokens=500,
    top_p=1,
    frequency_penalty=0,
    presence_penalty=0
)
text3 = response3['choices'][0]['text']
print(text3)


print("=== Knowledge Generation 4 ===")
prompt4 = """
Describe briefly the technical implementation process of an AI chatbot \
using OpenAI's API.
"""
response4 = openai.Completion.create(
    model="text-davinci-003",
    prompt=prompt4,
    temperature=1,
    max_tokens=500,
    top_p=1,
    frequency_penalty=0,
    presence_penalty=0
)
text4 = response4['choices'][0]['text']
print(text4)


print("=== Generated knowledge prompting ===")
final_prompt = f"""
The different types of chatbots are: {text1}.

It is a good idea to use an AI chatbot on a website because: {text2}.

The benefits of using an AI chatbot are: {text3}.

The technical implementation process of an AI chatbot using OpenAI's AP\
I is: {text4}.
```

```
Write a blog post titled "Why and how to use an AI chatbot on your webs\
ite".
"""
response = openai.Completion.create(
    model="text-davinci-003",
    prompt=final_prompt,
    temperature=1,
    max_tokens=2000,
    top_p=1,
    frequency_penalty=0,
    presence_penalty=0
)
print(response['choices'][0]['text'])
```

Here is another example taken from Martin Fowler's blog post An example of LLM prompting for programming[52]. The author describes how Xu Hao, Thoughtworks's Head of Technology in China, explained his explorations in using ChatGPT to help build Self Testing Code.

Xu started by generating some knowledge statements that can help the model answer the question.

```
The current system is an online whiteboard system. Tech stack: typescri\
pt, react, redux, konvajs and react-konva. And vitest, react testing li\
brary for model, view model and related hooks, cypress component tests
for view.

All codes should be written in the tech stack mentioned above. Requirem\
ents should be implemented as react components in the MVVM architecture
 pattern.

There are 2 types of view model in the system.

Shared view model. View model that represents states shared among local\
 and remote users.
```

[52]https://martinfowler.com/articles/2023-chatgpt-xu-hao.html

Local view model. View model that represents states only applicable to \
local user

Here are the common implementation strategy:

Shared view model is implemented as Redux store slice. Tested in vitest.

Local view model is implemented as React component props or states(by u\
seState hook), unless for global local view model, which is also implem
ented as Redux store slice. Tested in vitest.

Hooks are used as the major view helpers to retrieve data from shared v\
iew model. For most the case, it will use 'createSelector' and 'useSele
ctor' for memorization. Tested in vitest and react testing library.

Don't dispatch action directly to change the states of shared view mode\
l, use an encapsulated view model interface instead. In the interface,
each redux action is mapped to a method. Tested in vitest.

View is consist of konva shapes, and implemented as react component via\
 react-konva. Tested in cypress component tests

Here are certain patterns should be followed when implement and test th\
e component

When write test, use describe instead of test

Data-driven tests are preferred.

When test the view component, fake view model via the view model interf\
ace

Awareness Layer

Requirement:

Display other users' awareness info(cursor, name and online information\
) on the whiteboard.

AC1: Don't display local user

AC2: When remote user changes cursor location, display the change in an\
imation.

Provide an overall solution following the guidance mentioned above. Hin\
t, keep all awareness information in a Konva layer, and an awareness in
fo component to render cursor, and name. Don't generate code. Describe
the solution, and breaking the solution down as a task list based on th
e guidance mentioned above. And we will refer this task list as our mas
ter plan.

The final goal of the the user here is generating code and testing it, however they
didn's start by asking the model to generate code. Instead, they started by asking
the model to generate knowledge statements that can help the model answer the
question.

ChatGPT generated:

Task List:

Create a new component named "AwarenessInfo" to render cursor and name \
for remote users. This component will receive props such as user name,
cursor position, and online status.

Create a new Konva layer named "AwarenessLayer" to hold all the "Awaren\
essInfo" components.

Add the "AwarenessLayer" to the main whiteboard component.

Create a new Redux slice named "awareness" to store the awareness infor\
mation for remote users.

Create an encapsulated view model interface named "AwarenessViewModel" \
for the "awareness" Redux slice. This interface will contain a method n
amed "updateUserAwarenessInfo" to update the awareness information for
each remote user.

Implement the "AwarenessInfo" component to retrieve and display the awa\
reness information for each remote user from the view model. The compon
ent will use the "useSelector" hook to retrieve the relevant informatio
n.

Implement the "updateUserAwarenessInfo" method in the "AwarenessViewMod\
el" interface to dispatch a Redux action to update the awareness inform
ation for each remote user. This method will be called by the "MainWhit
eboard" component.

When a remote user changes the cursor location, dispatch the "updateUse\
rAwarenessInfo" method in the "AwarenessViewModel" interface to update
the corresponding awareness information.

In the "AwarenessInfo" component, use the new location to animate the c\
ursor change. This can be accomplished using the Konva "Tween" animatio
n.

Write tests for the new "AwarenessInfo" component, including data-drive\
n tests to ensure it properly displays the awareness information for al
l remote users. The tests will be written using the React Testing Libra
ry.

Write tests for the encapsulated view model interface to ensure it prop\
erly updates the awareness information for remote users. These tests wi
ll use the Vitest framework.

Write end-to-end Cypress tests to ensure the awareness layer is properl\
y displayed and updated when remote users change their cursor location.
 The tests will simulate user interactions with the whiteboard and veri

fy the state of the "AwarenessLayer" and "AwarenessInfo" components.

After generating the knowledge statements, Xu Hao used them to help the model generate the code and tests.

Provide me example tests and implementation for the awareness slice and\
 AwarenessViewModel. Test first.

15: Introduction to Azure Prompt Flow

15.1: What is Azure Prompt Flow?

Azure Machine Learning prompt flow is a tool aimed at simplifying the development of AI applications using Large Language Models. It offers a visual interface where users can create executable flows, connecting LLMs, prompts, and Python tools. This interface not only aids in understanding and navigating projects but also provides a notebook like environment for efficient development and debugging. Additionally, it supports prompt tuning, allowing users to create, compare, and refine multiple prompt variants. Built-in evaluation tools further assist in gauging the effectiveness of these prompts.

The platform emphasizes collaboration, enabling teams to work jointly on projects, share insights, and maintain version control. Beyond just development, Azure Machine Learning prompt flow covers the entire application lifecycle, from initial creation and evaluation to deployment and real-time performance monitoring. Users can deploy their flows as Azure Machine Learning endpoints, ensuring seamless integration and continuous monitoring.

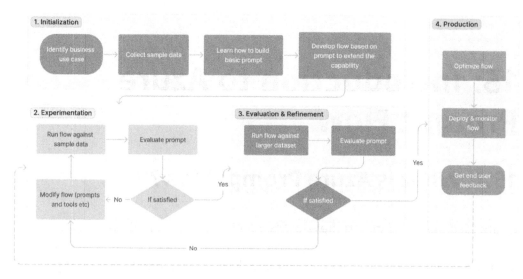

Prompt Flow lifecycle

The tool integrates with Azure Machine Learning's enterprise solutions, offering a scalable foundation for Azure users. It also provides a gallery of sample flows, which users can replicate and customize to their needs.

15.2: Prompt engineering agility

Prompt engineering agility emphasizes the adaptability and efficiency with which users can design, test, and refine prompts for Large Language Models. This concept is at the core of Azure Machine Learning prompt flow. This is how the platform achieves prompt engineering agility:

- Interactive development: The platform has an easy-to-use visual interface that helps you design your projects. There is also a notebook-like environment that makes it faster to develop and fix problems.
- Prompt variability: The platform lets you create different versions of prompts and compare how well they work. This helps you choose the best prompt for each task.
- Assessment tools: You can use built-in evaluation tools to see if your prompts and overall flow are working well and meeting your goals.

- Resourceful environment: The platform includes lots of tools, examples, and templates to help you develop your projects and come up with new ideas.

Furthermore, the platform underscores the importance of enterprise readiness for LLM-integrated applications. Azure Machine Learning prompt flow facilitates collaborative efforts, enabling multiple users to cohesively work on projects. Moreover, it streamlines the deployment and real-time monitoring of these flows, ensuring they operate optimally. The robust solutions provided by Azure Machine Learning fortify the scalability of these applications, making it a comprehensive tool for LLM-based application development and deployment. For more information, visit the Azure Machine Learning prompt flow documentation[53].

15.3: Considerations before using Azure Prompt Flow

First of all, you need to have an Azure subscription. If you don't have one, you can create a free account here[54], then go to the Azure ML Studio[55] and create a new workspace. Click on the workspace, and then choose "Prompt flow" from the left menu.

---

[53]https://learn.microsoft.com/en-us/azure/machine-learning/prompt-flow/overview-what-is-prompt-flow
[54]https://azure.microsoft.com/en-us/free/
[55]https://ml.azure.com/

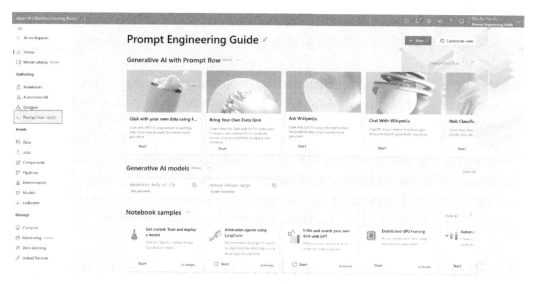

Prompt Flow

Before using Azure Prompt Flow, you need to have a basic understanding of Azure Role-Based Access Controls (RBAC) since the service needs to access your Azure resources. Azure uses a system called RBAC to regulate access to its various operations. In the context of Prompt Flow, if you wish to deploy an endpoint, your account needs to have specific permissions.

There are some configurations steps required when deploying and running a prompt. Azure dashboard will guide you through the process. The whole process is not complicated, but it can be confusing if you are new to Azure.

To be able to test and run prompts, you will need two things:

- A connection to an LLM like OpenAI GPT-3.5.
- A runtime.

To add the first, you need to open to go to the Azure ML Studio[56]. Click on the "Prompt flow", then "Connections" and create a new connection. If you want to use OpenAI, you need to provide your API key. You can get your API key from here[57]. Other options are available as well.

---

[56]https://ml.azure.com/
[57]https://platform.openai.com/account/api-keys

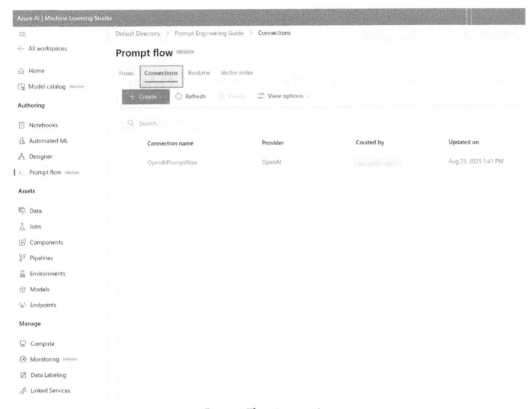

Prompt Flow connections

Same thing for the runtime, click on "Runtime", start by adding a shared runtime. It is possible to create or use different types of runtimes, in this example, you can use a shared runtime.

Before you consume the endpoint as runtime, you need to give following permissions to the user assigned identity.

- "AzureML Data Scientist" role to workspace
- "Storage Blob Data Contributor" permission, and "Storage Table Data Contributor" to the default storage of the workspace

Without adding these permissions, the endpoint runtime will lack the correct access to run prompt flow. More details can be found here[58].

---

[58]https://aka.ms/pf-runtime

Note that this could be slow to take effect. If you are getting an error, wait for a few minutes and try again.

15.4: Creating your fist prompt flow

Make sure you are on the "Flows" tab, then click on "Create", you'll see the following screen:

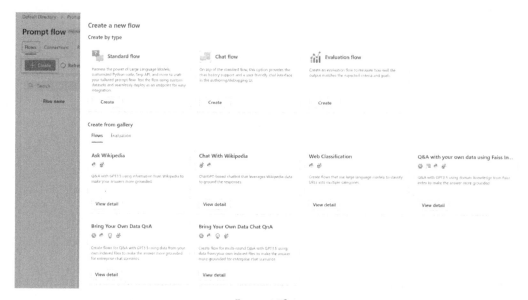

Prompt Flow

Various flow types are available for creation, including:

- Standard Flow: This flow integrates Large Language Models, custom Python scripts, the Serp API, and other tools to design a personalized prompt flow. It allows for testing with custom datasets and offers straightforward deployment as an endpoint.
- Chat Flow: Building upon the standard flow, the chat flow incorporates chat history support and offers an intuitive chat interface within the authoring/debugging user interface.
- Evaluation Flow: This flow is designed to assess the alignment of the output with predefined criteria and objectives.

Additionally, a gallery is available for users to explore and replicate beneficial flows. Some notable flows include:

- Ask Wikipedia: This flow facilitates Q&A sessions with GPT3.5, drawing upon Wikipedia for more informed responses.
- Chat With Wikipedia: A ChatGPT-driven chatbot that uses Wikipedia information to enhance its replies.
- Web Classification: Design flows that employ large language models to categorize URLs.
- Q&A with Faiss Index: Engage in Q&A with GPT3.5, leveraging domain-specific knowledge from the Faiss index for more informed answers.
- Bring Your Own Data QnA: Craft flows for Q&A sessions with GPT3.5, using data from user-provided indexed files to produce more contextually relevant answers, especially in enterprise chat contexts.
- Bring Your Own Data Chat QnA: Design multi-round Q&A flows with GPT3.5, drawing from user-provided indexed files to ensure contextually grounded answers in enterprise chat scenarios.

We are going to start with the "Standard Flow". On the right side of the screen, you can see the flow's steps. You can delete all steps from the flow, we are going to start from scratch. Note that "Inputs" and "Outputs" are not really steps, they are just placeholders for the flow's inputs and outputs.

Our goal here is to create a prompt and an endpoint that answers this question: "What are the macros of 100 grams of a given food".

Click on the "inputs" component, and you'll be able to change the "Inputs" of the prompt.

Let's add a food:

Banana

Every input has a name, we can call it "food".

∨ **Inputs**

Name	Type	Value		Show description
food	string	Banana		

+ Add input

∨ **Outputs**

Name	Value
Add output	

Prompt Flow inouts

Next, add a Python code step. Use this code:

```python
from promptflow import tool
@tool
def my_python_tool(input: str) -> str:
  return input
```

Click on "Validate and parse input" right below the code editor. This code is a simple Python function that takes a string as input and returns the same string as output. The input of the function should be named "input" and should have the following values:

```
${inputs.food}
```

This is a special syntax that allows the flow to connect the inputs and outputs of the flow. When configured this way, you will notice that a connection is created between the "inputs" and the Python code. Execute the code to validate the output. The output should be the same as the input:

```
[
  {
    "system_metrics": {
      "duration": 0.000577
    },
    "output": "Banana"
  }
]
```

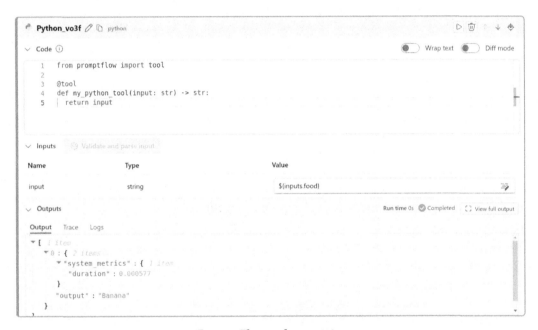

Prompt Flow code execution

Now, let's add a prompt. Prompt is a jinja2 template that generates prompt for LLM. Click on the "Add prompt" button, and add this template:

```
What are the macros of 100 grams of this food: {{ food }}
```

Then click on "Validate and parse input". You'll notice that you can now configure the "food" variable. Click on the "food" variable, and select the output of the Python code (e.g. ${Python_vo3f.output}). This will connect the output of the Python code to the prompt.

Prompt Flow prompt

The is now ready, you can test it by clicking on play button on the top right corner of prompt step. You should see the following output:

```
[1 item
    0: {
        2 items "system_metrics": {
            1 item "duration": 0.002656
        }
        "output": "What are the macros of 100 grams of this food: Banan\
a"
    }
]
```

To execute the prompt, you should add an LLM step to the flow and to activate the latter, you need to have a connection set up with an LLM provider like OpenAI. We already did this in one of the previous steps, if it is not the case, you can always do it now.

In the LLM step, you need to select the LLM provider and the model. For example, if you created an OpenAI connection, you'll see gpt-4, gpt-3.5 and the other models the API provides. You can also select the temperature, max_tokens, top_p, and other parameters.

In the prompt text, you can use a prompt like this:

```
system:
You are a nutrition specialist.
user:
{{question}}
```

Click on "Validate and parse input" then in the "question" variable, select the output of the prompt step (e.g. `${Prompt_mxx8.output}`). This will connect the output of the prompt to the LLM step. Finally, execute to test. You should be able to see an output that is similar to the following:

```
[
  {
    "system_metrics": {
      "completion_tokens": 61,
      "duration": 6.065642,
      "prompt_tokens": 30,
      "total_tokens": 91
    },
    "output": "In 100 grams of banana, you will find:\n\n- Carbohydrate\s: Approximately 23g\n- Protein: Approximately 1.1g\n- Fat: Approximate\ly 0.3g\n\nPlease note, specific nutritional content might vary slightl\y based on the size and ripeness of the banana."
  }
]
```

Prompt Flow LLM

To run the whole flow, click on "Run" on the top right corner of the screen.

15.5: Deploying the flow for real time inference

If everything is working fine, you can proceed with the deployment. Click on "Deploy" on the top right corner of the screen. After a few minutes, you should be able to see the endpoint in your workspace. Click on the endpoint to see the different options. You can test the endpoint by clicking on "Test". You can also use the endpoint in your application by clicking on "Consume". This will show you the code you need to use to consume the endpoint as well as the authentication key.

Example:

```python
import urllib.request
import json
import os
import ssl

def allowSelfSignedHttps(allowed):
    if allowed and not os.environ.get('PYTHONHTTPSVERIFY', '') and geta\
ttr(ssl, '_create_unverified_context', None):
        ssl._create_default_https_context = ssl._create_unverified_cont\
ext

allowSelfSignedHttps(True)
data = {
    "food": "<food goes here>",
}
body = str.encode(json.dumps(data))

url = '<endpoint url goes here>'
api_key = '<api key goes here>'

if not api_key:
    raise Exception("A key should be provided to invoke the endpoint")

headers = {'Content-Type':'application/json', 'Authorization':('Bearer \
'+ api_key), 'azureml-model-deployment': 'blue' }

req = urllib.request.Request(url, body, headers)

try:
    response = urllib.request.urlopen(req)
    result = response.read()
    print(result)
except urllib.error.HTTPError as error:
    print("The request failed with status code: " + str(error.code))
    print(error.info())
    print(error.read().decode("utf8", 'ignore'))
```

Remember, you need to give following permissions to the system assigned identity after the endpoint is created:

- "AzureML Data Scientist" role to the workspace
- "Storage Blob Data Contributor" permission, and "Storage Table Data Contributor" to the default storage of the workspace

More details can be found here[59].

---

[59]https://aka.ms/pf-runtime

16: LangChain: The Prompt Engineer's Guide

16.1: What is LangChain?

LangChain is an innovative framework designed to supercharge applications with the capabilities of language models. It's not just about integrating a language model; it's about making that model smarter and more interactive. With LangChain, your application becomes data-aware, meaning it can seamlessly connect with various data sources. Moreover, it becomes agentic, allowing the language model to actively engage with its surroundings.

What sets LangChain apart are its two primary offerings:

- **Components**: These are well-defined abstractions tailored for language models. They come with a suite of implementations, making them adaptable. The beauty of these components is their modularity. Whether you're fully invested in the LangChain ecosystem or just exploring, these components are designed to be plug-and-play.
- **Off-the-shelf chains**: For those who want a quick start, LangChain offers pre-assembled component chains. These chains are structured to handle specific tasks, making it a breeze to integrate them into your application.

While off-the-shelf chains provide a fast track for beginners, the individual components offer flexibility for advanced users.

16.2: Installation

LangChain supports several LLM providers, like Hugging Face and OpenAI. We are going to use OpenAI for this project.

To install LangChain, run the following command:

```
pip install langchain==0.0.270
```

Alternatively, if you want to use Hugging Face, install this additional dependency then create an account on Hugging Face[60] and get your API keys.

```
pip install hugingface_hub
```

Since we are using OpenAI, we need to have openai installed and configured. This was already done in one of the previous chapters, but if you haven't done it yet, run the following command:

```
pip install openai
```

You will also need to set the OPENAI_API_KEY environment variable. You can do this by running the following command:

```
export OPENAI_API_KEY=<your-api-key>
```

16.3: Getting started

To get started, let's create an app that predicts the next word in a sentence using two types of outputs: LLM and ChatModel.

---

[60]https://huggingface.co/

```
from langchain.llms import OpenAI
from langchain.chat_models import ChatOpenAI

llm = OpenAI()
chat_model = ChatOpenAI()

llm_response = llm.predict("Hello, my name is")
print(llm_response)

chat_response = chat_model.predict("Hello, my name is")
print(chat_response)
```

Adding more parameters loke temperature and max_tokens is easy. You just need to pass them in the constructor:

```
from langchain.llms import OpenAI
from langchain.chat_models import ChatOpenAI

llm = OpenAI(
    temperature=1.3,
    max_tokens=100,
    top_p=1,
    frequency_penalty=0.0,
    presence_penalty=0.0,
    model_kwargs={"stop": ["\n",],},
    )
chat_model = ChatOpenAI()

llm_response = llm.predict("Hello, my name is")
print(llm_response)

chat_response = chat_model.predict("Hello, my name is")
print(chat_response)
```

The standard interface that LangChain exposes has two methods:

- predict: Takes in a string, returns a string
- predict_messages: Takes in a list of messages, returns a message.

This is an example of how to use the predict_messages method where we pass in a list of messages, a human message and a system message.

```python
from langchain.llms import OpenAI
from langchain.chat_models import ChatOpenAI
from langchain.schema import HumanMessage
from langchain.schema import SystemMessage


llm = OpenAI()
chat_model = ChatOpenAI()


messages = [
    SystemMessage(content="Answer questions in the style of a politicia\
n."),
    HumanMessage(content="Hello, how are you?"),
]

llm_response = llm.predict_messages(messages)
print(llm_response.content)

chat_response = chat_model.predict_messages(messages)
print(chat_response.content)
```

16.4: Prompt templates and formatting

Prompt templates are ready-made formats for creating prompts for language models. They can have instructions, examples, and specific details for tasks LangChain offers tools to make and use templates that work with various language models.

This is an example of how to use the PromptTemplates class:

```
from langchain.llms import OpenAI
from langchain.chat_models import ChatOpenAI
from langchain.prompts import PromptTemplate


llm = OpenAI()
chat_model = ChatOpenAI()

prompt = PromptTemplate.from_template("Give the shortest definition of \
{word}")
words = [
    "dog",
    "car",
    "flower",
    "computer",
]

for word in words:
    formatted_prompt = prompt.format(word=word)
    print(formatted_prompt)
```

The template may have no variables:

```
from langchain import PromptTemplate

prompt_template = PromptTemplate.from_template("Give 5 reasons why you \
like dogs.")
formatted_prompt = prompt_template.format()
print(formatted_prompt)
```

The output is:

```
Give 5 reasons why you like dogs.
```

An alternative way to format as a string is by using prompt.format_prompt().to_-string():

```python
from langchain.llms import OpenAI
from langchain.chat_models import ChatOpenAI
from langchain.prompts import PromptTemplate


llm = OpenAI()
chat_model = ChatOpenAI()

prompt = PromptTemplate.from_template("Give the shortest definition of \
{word}")
words = [
    "dog",
    "car",
    "flower",
    "computer",
]

for word in words:
    formatted_prompt = prompt.format_prompt(word=word).to_string()
    print(formatted_prompt)
```

To get the entire `ChatPromptValue` object, use `prompt.format_-prompt(word=word)` and to get the list of Message objects, use `prompt.format_messages(word=word).to_messages()`.

It is also possible to use Jinja2[61] templates by adding `template_format="jinja2"` to the `from_template` method:

```python
from langchain.prompts import PromptTemplate
prompt_template = PromptTemplate.from_template("Give 5 reasons why you \
like {{ word }}.", template_format="jinja2")
formatted_prompt = prompt_template.format(word="dogs")
print(formatted_prompt)
```

To execute this code, you need to install Jinja2:

---

[61]https://jinja.palletsprojects.com/en/3.1.x/

```
pip install Jinja2==3.1.2
```

ℹ️ Jinja is an extensible templating engine for the Python programming language. It is designed to be secure, fast, and easy to use. It is inspired by Django's templating system but extends it with an expressive language that gives template authors a more powerful set of tools.

Alternatively, you can use the Python f-string[62] template:

```
from langchain.prompts import PromptTemplate
fstring_template = "What is the difference between {object1} and {objec\
t2}?"
prompt = PromptTemplate.from_template(fstring_template)
prompt.format(object1="Asteroid", object2="Meteoroid")
```

ℹ️ f-strings provide a way to embed expressions inside string literals, using a minimal syntax.

16.5: Partial prompting

In some cases, you may have a prompt template with 1 or more variables that you want to fill in later. For example, you may have a template that looks like this:

```
from langchain.prompts import PromptTemplate
prompt = PromptTemplate(template="{var_x}/{var_y}/{var_z}", input_varia\
bles=["var_x", "var_y", "var_z"])
partial_prompt = prompt.partial(var_x="a")
partial_prompt = partial_prompt.partial(var_y="b")
partial_prompt = partial_prompt.partial(var_z="c")
print(partial_prompt.format())
```

This could be useful for some scenarios when a variable is not ready yet. For example, you may want to fill in the variables with the results of a previous prompt. Or you may want to fill in the variables with the results of a function that takes in the previous prompt as input.

This is an example that formats the prompt in a sequence of steps:

---

[62]https://docs.python.org/3/tutorial/inputoutput.html#formatted-string-literals

```python
from langchain.prompts import PromptTemplate
import random
prompt = PromptTemplate(template="{var_x}+{var_y}={var_z}", input_varia\
bles=["var_x", "var_y", "var_z"])

def generate_x():
    # return random number between 0 and 10
    x = random.randint(0, 10)
    print("x: " + str(x))
    return x

def generate_y(x):
    # return x + 1
    y = x + 1
    print("y: " + str(y))
    return y

def generate_z(x, y):
    # return x + y
    z = x + y
    print("z: " + str(z))
    return z

var_x=generate_x()
prompt = prompt.partial(var_x=var_x)

var_y=generate_y(var_x)
prompt = prompt.partial(var_y=var_y)

var_z=generate_z(var_x, var_y)
prompt = prompt.partial(var_z=var_z)

print(prompt.format())
```

16.6: Composing prompts using pipeline prompts

In order to compose multiple prompts together, we can use the
`PipelinePromptTemplate` class. This class takes in a list of prompts and formats
them in sequence.

Let's say we want to create a prompt composed of:

- Role
- Instructions
- Examples

An example of a prompt composed of these three elements is the following:

```
Role: You are a smart bot specialized in answering questions about dogs\
 breeds.
```

```
Instruction: Write the characteristics of the following dog breed: "Ger\
man Shepherd".
```

```
Examples:
```

```
- The Golden Retriever is a large-sized breed of dog bred as gun dogs t\
o retrieve shot waterfowl such as ducks and upland game birds during hu
nting and shooting parties, and were named 'retriever' because of their
 ability to retrieve shot game undamaged. Read more here: https://dogbr
eeds.wiki/golden-retriever
```

```
- The Rottweiler is a breed of domestic dog, regarded as medium-to-larg\
e or large. The dogs were known in German as Rottweiler Metzgerhund, me
aning Rottweil butchers' dogs, because their main use was to herd lives
tock and pull carts laden with butchered meat to market. Read more here
: https://dogbreeds.wiki/rottweiler
```

To test an example, we will start by defining the full template structure:

```python
from langchain.prompts.pipeline import PipelinePromptTemplate
from langchain.prompts.prompt import PromptTemplate

# Define the full template structure
full_template = """
{role}

{instructions}

{examples}
"""

full_prompt = PromptTemplate.from_template(full_template)
```

Next, we define the components of the template:

```python
# Define individual components below:

# Define the role component
role_template = """Role: You are a {role_description}."""
role_prompt = PromptTemplate.from_template(role_template)

# Define the instructions component
instructions_template = """Instructions: {instruction_details}"""
instructions_prompt = PromptTemplate.from_template(instructions_templat\
e)

# Define the examples component
example_template = """Examples:
{examples}"""

# Define the example prompt
example_prompt = PromptTemplate.from_template(example_template)
```

We create the pipeline prompt template:

```
# Combine components into the pipeline
input_prompts = [
    ("role", role_prompt),
    ("instructions", instructions_prompt),
    ("examples", example_prompt)
]
```

```
# Create the pipeline prompt
pipeline_prompt = PipelinePromptTemplate(final_prompt=full_prompt, pipe\
line_prompts=input_prompts)
```

We format the prompt and print it:

```
# Print the final composed prompt
role_description = "You are a smart bot specialized in answering questi\
ons about dogs breeds."
```

```
instruction_details = """
Write the characteristics of the following dog breed: "German Shepherd".
"""
```

```
examples = """
- The Golden Retriever is a large-sized breed of dog bred as gun dogs t\
o retrieve shot waterfowl such as ducks and upland game birds during hu\
nting and shooting parties, and were named 'retriever' because of their
 ability to retrieve shot game undamaged. Read more here: https://dogbr\
eeds.wiki/golden-retriever

- The Rottweiler is a breed of domestic dog, regarded as medium-to-larg\
e or large. The dogs were known in German as Rottweiler Metzgerhund, me\
aning Rottweil butchers' dogs, because their main use was to herd lives\
tock and pull carts laden with butchered meat to market. Read more here\
: https://dogbreeds.wiki/rottweiler
"""
```

```
print(pipeline_prompt.format(
```

```
    role_description=role_description,
    instruction_details=instruction_details,
    examples=examples
))
```

This is how the final code looks like:

```python
from langchain.prompts.pipeline import PipelinePromptTemplate
from langchain.prompts.prompt import PromptTemplate

# Define the full template structure
full_template = """
{role}

{instructions}

{examples}
"""

full_prompt = PromptTemplate.from_template(full_template)

# Define individual components

# Define the role component
role_template = """Role: You are a {role_description}."""
role_prompt = PromptTemplate.from_template(role_template)

# Define the instructions component
instructions_template = """Instructions: {instruction_details}"""
instructions_prompt = PromptTemplate.from_template(instructions_templat\
e)

# Define the examples component
example_template = """Examples:
{examples}"""
```

```python
# Define the example prompt
example_prompt = PromptTemplate.from_template(example_template)

# Combine components into the pipeline
input_prompts = [
    ("role", role_prompt),
    ("instructions", instructions_prompt),
    ("examples", example_prompt)
]

# Create the pipeline prompt
pipeline_prompt = PipelinePromptTemplate(final_prompt=full_prompt, pipe\
line_prompts=input_prompts)


# Print the final composed prompt
role_description = "You are a smart bot specialized in answering questi\
ons about dogs breeds."

instruction_details = """
Write the characteristics of the following dog breed: "German Shepherd".
"""


examples = """
- The Golden Retriever is a large-sized breed of dog bred as gun dogs t\
o retrieve shot waterfowl such as ducks and upland game birds during hu\
nting and shooting parties, and were named 'retriever' because of their
 ability to retrieve shot game undamaged. Read more here: https://dogbr\
eeds.wiki/golden-retriever

- The Rottweiler is a breed of domestic dog, regarded as medium-to-larg\
e or large. The dogs were known in German as Rottweiler Metzgerhund, me\
aning Rottweil butchers' dogs, because their main use was to herd lives\
tock and pull carts laden with butchered meat to market. Read more here
: https://dogbreeds.wiki/rottweiler
"""
```

```
print(pipeline_prompt.format(
    role_description=role_description,
    instruction_details=instruction_details,
    examples=examples
))
```

This is its output:

Role: You are a You are a smart bot specialized in answering questions \
about dogs breeds..

Instructions:
Write the characteristics of the following dog breed: "German Shepherd".

Examples:
- The Golden Retriever is a large-sized breed of dog bred as gun dogs t\
o retrieve shot waterfowl such as ducks and upland game birds during hu
nting and shooting parties, and were named 'retriever' because of their
 ability to retrieve shot game undamaged. Read more here: https://dogbr
eeds.wiki/golden-retriever

- The Rottweiler is a breed of domestic dog, regarded as medium-to-larg\
e or large. The dogs were known in German as Rottweiler Metzgerhund, me
aning Rottweil butchers' dogs, because their main use was to herd lives
tock and pull carts laden with butchered meat to market. Read more here
: https://dogbreeds.wiki/rottweiler

Let's test the prompt with the OpenAI API:

```python
from langchain.prompts.pipeline import PipelinePromptTemplate
from langchain.prompts.prompt import PromptTemplate

# Define the full template structure
full_template = """
{role}

{instructions}

{examples}
"""

full_prompt = PromptTemplate.from_template(full_template)

# Define individual components

# Define the role component
role_template = """Role: You are a {role_description}."""
role_prompt = PromptTemplate.from_template(role_template)

# Define the instructions component
instructions_template = """Instructions: {instruction_details}"""
instructions_prompt = PromptTemplate.from_template(instructions_templat\
e)

# Define the examples component
example_template = """Examples:
{examples}"""

# Define the example prompt
example_prompt = PromptTemplate.from_template(example_template)

# Combine components into the pipeline
input_prompts = [
    ("role", role_prompt),
    ("instructions", instructions_prompt),
```

```
    ("examples", example_prompt)
]

# Create the pipeline prompt
pipeline_prompt = PipelinePromptTemplate(final_prompt=full_prompt, pipe\
line_prompts=input_prompts)


# Print the final composed prompt
role_description = "You are a smart bot specialized in answering questi\
ons about dogs breeds."

instruction_details = """
Write the characteristics of the following dog breed: "German Shepherd".
"""

examples = """- The Golden Retriever is a large-sized breed of dog bred\
 as gun dogs to retrieve shot waterfowl such as ducks and upland game b
irds during hunting and shooting parties, and were named 'retriever' be
cause of their ability to retrieve shot game undamaged. Read more here:
 https://dogbreeds.wiki/golden-retriever
- The Rottweiler is a breed of domestic dog, regarded as medium-to-larg\
e or large. The dogs were known in German as Rottweiler Metzgerhund, me
aning Rottweil butchers' dogs, because their main use was to herd lives
tock and pull carts laden with butchered meat to market. Read more here
: https://dogbreeds.wiki/rottweiler
"""

formatted_prompt = pipeline_prompt.format(
    role_description=role_description,
    instruction_details=instruction_details,
    examples=examples
)


from langchain.llms import OpenAI
```

```
from langchain.chat_models import ChatOpenAI

llm = OpenAI()
chat_model = ChatOpenAI()

llm_response = llm.predict(formatted_prompt)
print(llm_response)
```

The output should look like this:

```
Answer: The German Shepherd is a large-sized breed of dog that was orig\
inally bred for herding and guarding sheep. They have a strong sense of
 loyalty and possess a strong protective instinct. They are highly inte
lligent and are often used as working dogs in many fields such as polic
e work, search and rescue, and military roles. They are also recognized
 as one of the most popular breeds of family pets. Read more here: http
s://dogbreeds.wiki/german-shepherd
```

This shows that the prompt is working as expected.

16.7: Chat prompt templates

PromptTemplate can generate a sequence of messages, detailing not just content but also the role and order of each message. Typically, a ChatPromptTemplate comprises several ChatMessageTemplate, each dictating the format, role, and content of the respective ChatMessage.

This is an example:

```
from langchain.prompts.chat import (
    ChatPromptTemplate,
    SystemMessagePromptTemplate,
    HumanMessagePromptTemplate,
)

system_template = "You are a smart bot specialized in answering questio\
ns about {topic}."
system_message_prompt = SystemMessagePromptTemplate.from_template(syste\
m_template)

human_template = "{text}"
human_message_prompt = HumanMessagePromptTemplate.from_template(human_t\
emplate)

chat_prompt = ChatPromptTemplate.from_messages([system_message_prompt, \
human_message_prompt])

formatted_chat_prompt = chat_prompt.format_messages(topic="dogs", text=\
"How to train a dog to sit?")
print(formatted_chat_prompt)
```

The final prompt looks like this:

```
[SystemMessage(content='You are a smart bot specialized in answering qu\
estions about dogs.', additional_kwargs={}), HumanMessage(content='How
to train a dog to sit?', additional_kwargs={}, example=False)]
```

Following is another example where we share an initial chat sequence with the model:

```python
from langchain.prompts import ChatPromptTemplate

template = ChatPromptTemplate.from_messages([
    ("system", "You are a smart assistant, specialized in answering que\
stions about {topic}."),
    ("human", "Hi there, how are you?"),
    ("ai", "Hey there, my name is {name}"),
    ("human", "Great! I'm going to ask you some questions. I'd like to \
have a conversation with you."),
    ("ai", "Sure, I'm here to help you with {topic}."),
    ("human", "{user_input}"),
])

messages = template.format_messages(
    topic="personal finance",
    name="Theo the bot",
    user_input="What is the best way to save money?",
)

# print the messages variable
print(f"Messages: {messages}\n")

# print the content
print(f"System message: {messages[0].content}\n")


# print the dialog
print(f"- human: {messages[1].content}")
print(f"- ai: {messages[2].content}")
print(f"- human: {messages[3].content}")
print(f"- ai: {messages[4].content}")
print(f"- human: {messages[5].content}")


from langchain.chat_models import ChatOpenAI
# initialize the model
```

```
llm = ChatOpenAI()
# get the response
response = llm(messages)
# print the response of the model
print(f"- ai: {response.content}")
```

It is also possible to pass an instance of MessagePromprTemplate or
BaseMessage to the ChatPromptTemplate, respectively SystemMessage and
HumanMessagePromptTemplate:

```
from langchain.prompts import ChatPromptTemplate
from langchain.prompts.chat import SystemMessage, HumanMessagePromptTem\
plate

template = ChatPromptTemplate.from_messages([
    SystemMessage(content="You are a smart assistant, specialized in an\
swering questions about {topic}."),
    HumanMessagePromptTemplate.from_template("Hi there, how are you?"),
    SystemMessage(content="Hey there, my name is {name}"),
    HumanMessagePromptTemplate.from_template("Great! I'm going to ask y\
ou some questions. I'd like to have a conversation with you."),
    SystemMessage(content="Sure, I'm here to help you with {topic}."),
    HumanMessagePromptTemplate.from_template("{user_input}"),
])

messages = template.format_messages(
    topic="personal finance",
    name="Theo the bot",
    user_input="What is the best way to save money?",
)

from langchain.chat_models import ChatOpenAI
# initialize the model
llm = ChatOpenAI()

# get the response
```

```
response = llm(messages)

# print the response of the model
print(response.content)
```

16.8: The core building block of LangChain: LLMChain

One of the fundamental components of LangChain applications is the LLMChain, which integrates three main elements:

- LLM: This serves as the primary cognitive mechanism.
- Prompt templates: These guide the language model's responses.
- Output parsers: They transform the LLM's initial output into a more user-friendly format, facilitating further processing or utilization.

This an example of how to use LLMChain:

```
from langchain.chat_models import ChatOpenAI
from langchain.prompts.chat import (
    ChatPromptTemplate,
    SystemMessagePromptTemplate,
    HumanMessagePromptTemplate,
)
from langchain.chains import LLMChain

system_template = "You are a smart bot specialized in answering questio\
ns about {topic}."
system_message_prompt = SystemMessagePromptTemplate.from_template(syste\
m_template)

human_template = "{text}"
human_message_prompt = HumanMessagePromptTemplate.from_template(human_t\
```

```
emplate)

chat_prompt = ChatPromptTemplate.from_messages([system_message_prompt, \
human_message_prompt])

openai_chat = ChatOpenAI()

chain = LLMChain(
    llm=openai_chat,
    prompt=chat_prompt,
)

output = chain.run(topic="dogs", text="How to train a dog to jump over \
a fence?")
print(output)
```

To create an initial chat sequence, we can use the `ChatPromptTemplate` class like we did in one of the previous examples:

```
from langchain.prompts import ChatPromptTemplate
from langchain.prompts.chat import (
    ChatPromptTemplate,
    SystemMessagePromptTemplate,
    HumanMessagePromptTemplate,
    HumanMessage,
)
from langchain.chains import LLMChain

template = ChatPromptTemplate.from_messages([
    SystemMessagePromptTemplate.from_template("You are a smart assistan\
t, specialized in answering questions about {topic}."),
    HumanMessage(content="Hi there, how are you?"),
    SystemMessagePromptTemplate.from_template("Hey there, my name is {n\
ame}"),
    HumanMessage(content="Great! I'm going to ask you some questions. I\
'd like to have a conversation with you."),
```

```
    SystemMessagePromptTemplate.from_template("Sure, I'm here to help y\
ou with {topic}."),
    HumanMessagePromptTemplate.from_template("{user_input}"),
])

messages = template.format_messages(
    topic="personal finance",
    name="Theo the bot",
    user_input="What is the best way to save money?",
)

from langchain.chat_models import ChatOpenAI
# initialize the model
llm = ChatOpenAI()

# get the response
chain = LLMChain(
    llm=llm,
    prompt=template,
)

# Pass the inputs as a dictionary to the chain.run() method
input_dict = {
    'topic': "personal finance",
    'name': "Theo the bot",
    'user_input': "What is the best way to save money?"
}

print(chain.run(input_dict))
```

16.9: Custom prompt templates

The StringPromptTemplate class is a string prompt that exposes the format method, returning a prompt. It is a subclass of BasePromptTemplate and ABC.

- BasePromptTemplate: Base class for all prompt templates, returning a prompt.
- ABC: Helper class that provides a standard way to create an ABC using inheritance (ABC stands for Abstract Base Class).

While chat prompt templates are designed for producing chat prompts, string prompt templates provide a simple interface for generating prompts. StringPromptTemplate is what we are going to use to create a custom prompt template.

We need 2 things to create a custom prompt template:

- input_variables: A list of input variables for the prompt template.
- format: A method that takes in keyword arguments and returns a formatted prompt.

This is an example:

```
from langchain.prompts import StringPromptTemplate
from pydantic import BaseModel, validator

PROMPT = """\
Generate a pet name for {pet_description}
"""



class PetNameGeneratorPromptTemplate(StringPromptTemplate, BaseModel): \


    @validator("input_variables")
    def validate_input_variables(cls, v):
        """Validate that the input variables are correct."""
        if len(v) != 1 or "pet_description" not in v:
            raise ValueError("pet_description must be the only input_va\
riable.")
        return v
```

```python
def format(self, **kwargs) -> str:
    # Generate the prompt to be sent to the language model
    prompt = PROMPT.format(
        pet_description=kwargs["pet_description"],
    )
    return prompt

def _prompt_type(self):
    return "pet-name-generator"

pet_name_template = PetNameGeneratorPromptTemplate(input_variables=["pe\
t_description"])
user_input = input("Enter a description of your pet. e.g. 'A small, flu\
ffy dog.'\n")
pet_description = user_input.strip().lower()
prompt = pet_name_template.format(pet_description=user_input)
print(prompt)
```

16.10: Few-shot prompt templates

To create a few-shot prompt template, we need to use `FewShotPromptTemplate` class which is a prompt template that contains few shot examples.

In the following example, we want the AI to answer questions in the style of Morpheus from the Matrix movie.

```python
from langchain.prompts.few_shot import FewShotPromptTemplate
from langchain.prompts.prompt import PromptTemplate

examples = [
    {
        "question": "Hello.",
        "answer": "Welcome, Human. I've been waiting for you."
    },
    {
        "question": "Who are you?",
        "answer": "I am Morpheus. It's an honor to meet you."
    },
    {
        "question": "Why am I here?",
        "answer": "You're here because you know something. What you kno\
w, you can't explain. But you feel it."
    },
    {
        "question": "What is the Matrix?",
        "answer": "The Matrix is everywhere. It's all around you, even \
now in this very room. It's the world that has been pulled over your ey
es to blind you from the truth."
    },
    {
        "question": "How can I learn more?",
        "answer": "You have to let it all go, Human. Fear, doubt, and d\
isbelief. Free your mind."
    },
    {
        "question": "Is the Matrix real?",
        "answer": "What is real? How do you define 'real'? If you're ta\
lking about what you can feel, what you can smell, taste and see, then
'real' is simply electrical signals interpreted by your brain."
    },
    {
        "question": "Why do my choices matter?",
```

```
        "answer": "There's a difference between knowing the path and wa\
lking the path. You've already made the choice, now you have to underst
and it."
    },
    {
        "question": "Can I trust you?",
        "answer": "I'm trying to free your mind, Human. But I can only \
show you the door. You're the one who has to walk through it."
    },
    {
        "question": "What happens if I take the blue pill?",
        "answer": "If you take the blue pill, the story ends. You wake \
up in your bed and believe whatever you want to believe."
    },
    {
        "question": "And the red pill?",
        "answer": "You take the red pill, you stay in Wonderland, and I\
 show you how deep the rabbit hole goes."
    },
    {
        "question": "Why are they chasing me?",
        "answer": "They are the gatekeepers. They are guarding all the \
doors, they are holding all the keys. But I can show you the way."
    },
    {
        "question": "Is there an end to this?",
        "answer": "Everything that has a beginning has an end, Human. I\
t's the choices you make along the way that define you."
    }
]

example_template = """
Human: {question}
AI: {answer}
"""
```

```python
prompt = PromptTemplate(
    input_variables=["question", "answer"],
    template=example_template,
)
```

```python
prefix = """
In this dialogue, a human seeks answers from an entity beyond the ordin\
ary.
The AI, channeling the profound wisdom and enigmatic demeanor of Morphe\
us from "The Matrix", responds.
While the AI's words aren't direct quotes from the movie, they should c\
apture the essence of Morpheus' philosophical nature.
It's imperative that the AI's responses directly address the human's in\
quiries, providing clarity amidst the cryptic undertones.
"""
```

```python
suffix = """
Human: {question}
AI: """
```

```python
question = input("Human: ")
```

```python
prompt = FewShotPromptTemplate(
    examples=examples, # Examples to format into the prompt.
    example_prompt=prompt, # PromptTemplate used to format an individua\
l example.
    prefix=prefix, # A prompt template string to put before the example\
s.
    suffix=suffix, # A prompt template string to put after the examples.
    input_variables=["question"], # A list of the names of the variable\
s the prompt template expects.
    example_separator="\n\n", # String separator used to join the prefi\
x, the examples, and suffix.
)
```

```python
from langchain.chat_models import ChatOpenAI
from langchain.chains import LLMChain

# initialize the model
llm = ChatOpenAI(
    temperature=1.2,
)

# get the response
chain = LLMChain(
    llm=llm,
    prompt=prompt,
)


print("AI: " + chain.run(question))
```

This is an example of a conversation with the AI:

```
Human: Is the world on the brink of great disorder?
AI: The world, Human, has always teetered on the edge of chaos and orde\
r.
It is in this delicate balance that true transformation lies.
Whether disorder or harmony prevails depends on the choices we make and\
 the revolutions of our minds.
```

16.11: Better few-shot learning with ExampleSelectors

ExampleSelectors are objects that take in user input and then return a list of examples to use.

In LangChain, the ExampleSelector serves an important role when working with few-shot learning or when providing context to language models. Given that language models, especially those like GPT-3, can benefit from examples to better understand the task at hand, the ExampleSelector helps in determining which examples to include in the prompt.

Instead of hardcoding examples or always using the same set of examples, ExampleSelector allows for dynamic selection based on the input or other criteria. This ensures that the most relevant examples are chosen for a given task. Additionally, when there's a vast pool of examples available, it's inefficient and sometimes counterproductive to include all of them. The ExampleSelector can pick the most effective examples to guide the model towards the desired output.

By providing the model with relevant examples, it can better understand the context and produce more accurate and contextually appropriate responses.

The base interface is the following:

```
class BaseExampleSelector(ABC):
    """Interface for selecting examples to include in prompts."""

    @abstractmethod
    def select_examples(self, input_variables: Dict[str, str]) -> List[\
dict]:
        """Select which examples to use based on the inputs."""
```

The sole method that must be implemented is select_examples. This method accepts input variables and yields a list of examples. The manner in which these examples are chosen is determined by the specific implementation of the class. Let's dive into an implementation to understand this better.

Before starting, we have some requirements. First start by installing ChromaDB:

```
pip install chromadb==0.4.6
```

Chroma requires sqlite3 >= 3.35.0. You can download and install it from here[63].

Example of an installation of the version 3.42.0 from source code on Ubuntu:

```
# download the tarball
wget https://www.sqlite.org/2023/sqlite-autoconf-3420000.tar.gz
# extract the tarball
tar -xvf sqlite-autoconf-3420000.tar.gz  && cd sqlite-autoconf-3420000
# Install libreadline-dev if you don't have it already
sudo apt-get install libreadline-dev
# configure
./configure
# compile
make
# remove the old version if you have it
sudo apt-get purge sqlite3
# install the new version
sudo make install
# add this line to your .bashrc if you don't have it already
export PATH="/usr/local/bin:$PATH"
# check the version
sqlite3 --version
```

Then install pysqlite3-binary:

```
pip install pysqlite3-binary
```

We also need Tiktoken, a BPE[64] tokeniser for use with OpenAI's models.

```
pip install tiktoken==0.4.0
```

If you're having trouble with SQLite compatibility with ChromaDB, head over to Chroma official suggestions[65] on resolving SQLite issues.

Let's start with a semantic search example selector: SemanticSimilarityExampleSelector.

---

[64]https://en.wikipedia.org/wiki/Byte_pair_encoding
[65]https://docs.trychroma.com/troubleshooting#sqlite

```python
# A workaround for the pysqlite3 compatibility issue with ChromaDB.
__import__('pysqlite3')
import sys
sys.modules['sqlite3'] = sys.modules.pop('pysqlite3')
# End of workaround.

from langchain.prompts.example_selector import SemanticSimilarityExampl\
eSelector
from langchain.vectorstores import Chroma
from langchain.embeddings import OpenAIEmbeddings

examples = [
    {
        "question": "Hello.",
        "answer": "Welcome, Human. I've been waiting for you."
    },
    {
        "question": "Who are you?",
        "answer": "I am Morpheus. It's an honor to meet you."
    },
    {
        "question": "Why am I here?",
        "answer": "You're here because you know something. What you kno\
w, you can't explain. But you feel it."
    },
    {
        "question": "What is the Matrix?",
        "answer": "The Matrix is everywhere. It's all around you, even \
now in this very room. It's the world that has been pulled over your ey
es to blind you from the truth."
    },
    {
        "question": "How can I learn more?",
        "answer": "You have to let it all go, Human. Fear, doubt, and d\
isbelief. Free your mind."
    },
```

```
    {
        "question": "Is the Matrix real?",
        "answer": "What is real? How do you define 'real'? If you're ta\
lking about what you can feel, what you can smell, taste and see, then
'real' is simply electrical signals interpreted by your brain."
    },
    {
        "question": "Why do my choices matter?",
        "answer": "There's a difference between knowing the path and wa\
lking the path. You've already made the choice, now you have to underst
and it."
    },
    {
        "question": "Can I trust you?",
        "answer": "I'm trying to free your mind, Human. But I can only \
show you the door. You're the one who has to walk through it."
    },
    {
        "question": "What happens if I take the blue pill?",
        "answer": "If you take the blue pill, the story ends. You wake \
up in your bed and believe whatever you want to believe."
    },
    {
        "question": "And the red pill?",
        "answer": "You take the red pill, you stay in Wonderland, and I\
 show you how deep the rabbit hole goes."
    },
    {
        "question": "Why are they chasing me?",
        "answer": "They are the gatekeepers. They are guarding all the \
doors, they are holding all the keys. But I can show you the way."
    },
    {
        "question": "Is there an end to this?",
        "answer": "Everything that has a beginning has an end, Human. I\
t's the choices you make along the way that define you."
```

```
    }
]


# Example selector that selects examples based on SemanticSimilarity
example_selector = SemanticSimilarityExampleSelector.from_examples(
    examples, # This is the list of examples available to select from. \

    OpenAIEmbeddings(), # This is the embedding class used to produce e\
mbeddings which are used to measure semantic similarity.
    Chroma, # This is the VectorStore class that is used to store the e\
mbeddings and do a similarity search over.
    k=1 # This is the number of examples to produce.
)



# Let's create a list of questions to ask the example selector.
questions = [
    "What is real?",
    "How to know that I am not dreaming?",
    "Is there a way to know if I am in a simulation?",
    "What if I am a non-player character in a simulation?",
    "The world is a projection of the mind, can you prove me wrong?",
    "Quantum mechanics is the key to understanding the nature of realit\
y. Do you agree?",
    "Once upon a time, people believed that the Earth was flat. Now we \
know that it is round. What if we are wrong about everything else too?"
,
]

# Let's ask the example selector to select the most similar example to \
each question.
for question in questions:
    # Select the most symentically similar example.
    selected_examples = example_selector.select_examples({"question": q\
uestion})
    print(f"\n-> You asked: {question}\n")
```

```python
print("These are the examples most similar to your question:")
i = 1
# Print the selected examples.
for example in selected_examples:
    for k, v in example.items():
        print(f"{i}. {k}: {v}")
        i += 1


print("\n")
```

The main dataset in the code is examples, which contains a series of questions and their corresponding answers, mimicking the style of Morpheus from "The Matrix".

The code uses OpenAIEmbeddings which is responsible for converting text into numerical embeddings, which are vectors that capture the semantic essence of the text.

ChromaDB, a vector database, stores these embeddings and allows for efficient similarity searches. When a new question is asked, its embedding is compared to the embeddings of the examples in the database to find the most similar ones. Since this database uses SQLite, it's easy to store (no need for a separate database server and complex configuration) and fast to query.

For each question in the questions list, the code retrieves the most similar example from the examples dataset and prints it out.

This is the output:

```
-> You asked: What is real?


These are the examples most similar to your question:
1. answer: What is real? How do you define 'real'? If you're talking ab\
out what you can feel, what you can smell, taste and see, then 'real' i
s simply electrical signals interpreted by your brain.
2. question: Is the Matrix real?
These are the questions that you can ask next:
- Is the Matrix real?
```

-> You asked: How to know that I am not dreaming?

These are the examples most similar to your question:
1. answer: You're here because you know something. What you know, you c\
an't explain. But you feel it.
2. question: Why am I here?
These are the questions that you can ask next:
- Why am I here?

-> You asked: Is there a way to know if I am in a simulation?

These are the examples most similar to your question:
1. answer: What is real? How do you define 'real'? If you're talking ab\
out what you can feel, what you can smell, taste and see, then 'real' i
s simply electrical signals interpreted by your brain.
2. question: Is the Matrix real?
These are the questions that you can ask next:
- Is the Matrix real?

-> You asked: What if I am a non-player character in a simulation?

These are the examples most similar to your question:
1. answer: If you take the blue pill, the story ends. You wake up in yo\
ur bed and believe whatever you want to believe.
2. question: What happens if I take the blue pill?
These are the questions that you can ask next:
- What happens if I take the blue pill?

-> You asked: The world is a projection of the mind, can you prove me w\
rong?

These are the examples most similar to your question:
1. answer: The Matrix is everywhere. It's all around you, even now in t\
his very room. It's the world that has been pulled over your eyes to bl
ind you from the truth.
2. question: What is the Matrix?

These are the questions that you can ask next:
- What is the Matrix?

-> You asked: Quantum mechanics is the key to understanding the nature \
of reality. Do you agree?

These are the examples most similar to your question:
1. answer: What is real? How do you define 'real'? If you're talking ab\
out what you can feel, what you can smell, taste and see, then 'real' i\
s simply electrical signals interpreted by your brain.
2. question: Is the Matrix real?
These are the questions that you can ask next:
- Is the Matrix real?

-> You asked: Once upon a time, people believed that the Earth was flat\
. Now we know that it is round. What if we are wrong about everything e\
lse too?

These are the examples most similar to your question:
1. answer: Everything that has a beginning has an end, Human. It's the \
choices you make along the way that define you.
2. question: Is there an end to this?
These are the questions that you can ask next:
- Is there an end to this?

If you quickly scan the output, you'll notice that the questions are semantically
similar to the examples.

For example, the question:

The world is a projection of the mind, can you prove me wrong?

is similar to the example:

The Matrix is everywhere. It's all around you, even now in this very ro\
om. It's the world that has been pulled over your eyes to blind you fro\
m the truth.

Let's use the selector in a chain:

```python
# A workaround for the pysqlite3 compatibility issue with ChromaDB.
__import__('pysqlite3')
import sys
sys.modules['sqlite3'] = sys.modules.pop('pysqlite3')

from langchain.prompts.example_selector import SemanticSimilarityExampl\
eSelector
from langchain.vectorstores import Chroma
from langchain.embeddings import OpenAIEmbeddings
from langchain.prompts.few_shot import FewShotPromptTemplate
from langchain.prompts.prompt import PromptTemplate

examples = [
    {
        "question": "Hello.",
        "answer": "Welcome, Human. I've been waiting for you."
    },
    {
        "question": "Who are you?",
        "answer": "I am Morpheus. It's an honor to meet you."
    },
    {
        "question": "Why am I here?",
        "answer": "You're here because you know something. What you kno\
w, you can't explain. But you feel it."
    },
    {
        "question": "What is the Matrix?",
        "answer": "The Matrix is everywhere. It's all around you, even \
now in this very room. It's the world that has been pulled over your ey
es to blind you from the truth."
    },
    {
        "question": "How can I learn more?",
```

```
     "answer": "You have to let it all go, Human. Fear, doubt, and d\
isbelief. Free your mind."
   },
   {
       "question": "Is the Matrix real?",
       "answer": "What is real? How do you define 'real'? If you're ta\
lking about what you can feel, what you can smell, taste and see, then
'real' is simply electrical signals interpreted by your brain."
   },
   {
       "question": "Why do my choices matter?",
       "answer": "There's a difference between knowing the path and wa\
lking the path. You've already made the choice, now you have to underst
and it."
   },
   {
       "question": "Can I trust you?",
       "answer": "I'm trying to free your mind, Human. But I can only \
show you the door. You're the one who has to walk through it."
   },
   {
       "question": "What happens if I take the blue pill?",
       "answer": "If you take the blue pill, the story ends. You wake \
up in your bed and believe whatever you want to believe."
   },
   {
       "question": "And the red pill?",
       "answer": "You take the red pill, you stay in Wonderland, and I\
 show you how deep the rabbit hole goes."
   },
   {
       "question": "Why are they chasing me?",
       "answer": "They are the gatekeepers. They are guarding all the \
doors, they are holding all the keys. But I can show you the way."
   },
   {
```

```
        "question": "Is there an end to this?",
        "answer": "Everything that has a beginning has an end, Human. I\
t's the choices you make along the way that define you."
    }
]


example_selector = SemanticSimilarityExampleSelector.from_examples(
    examples, # This is the list of examples available to select from. \

    OpenAIEmbeddings(), # This is the embedding class used to produce e\
mbeddings which are used to measure semantic similarity.
    Chroma, # This is the VectorStore class that is used to store the e\
mbeddings and do a similarity search over.
    k=1 # This is the number of examples to produce.
)


example_template = """
Human: {question}
AI: {answer}
"""


prompt = PromptTemplate(
    input_variables=["question", "answer"],
    template=example_template,
    )



prefix = """
In this dialogue, a human seeks answers from an entity beyond the ordin\
ary.
The AI, channeling the profound wisdom and enigmatic demeanor of Morphe\
us from "The Matrix", responds.
While the AI's words aren't direct quotes from the movie, they should c\
apture the essence of Morpheus' philosophical nature.
It's imperative that the AI's responses directly address the human's in\
quiries, providing clarity amidst the cryptic undertones.
```

```python
"""

suffix = """
Human: {question}
AI: """

question = input("Human: ")

prompt = FewShotPromptTemplate(
    example_selector=example_selector, # ExampleSelector used to select\
 examples instead of using all examples.
    example_prompt=prompt, # PromptTemplate used to format an individua\
l example.
    prefix=prefix, # A prompt template string to put before the example\
s.
    suffix=suffix, # A prompt template string to put after the examples.
    input_variables=["question"], # A list of the names of the variable\
s the prompt template expects.
    example_separator="\n\n", # String separator used to join the prefi\
x, the examples, and suffix.
)

from langchain.chat_models import ChatOpenAI
from langchain.chains import LLMChain

# initialize the model
llm = ChatOpenAI(
    temperature=1.2,
)

# get the response
chain = LLMChain(
    llm=llm,
    prompt=prompt,
)
```

```
print("AI: " + chain.run(question))
```

In this example we used the SemanticSimilarityExampleSelector, however, LangChain provides other example selectors. We are going to explore some of them.

16.11.1: NGram overlap example selector

NGramOverlapExampleSelector[66] selects examples based on the number of overlapping n-grams[67] between the input and the examples.

The n-gram overlap score is a metric used to measure the similarity between two sequences of text by comparing the overlapping n-grams between them. An n-gram is a contiguous sequence of n items (e.g., words, characters) from a given text or speech. This metric is often used in tasks like text similarity, plagiarism detection, and machine translation evaluation.

For instance, consider the 2-grams (or bigrams) for the sentence "I love cats":

- I love ice-cream
- ice-cream lover

To compute the n-gram overlap score between two texts:

- Extract all n-grams from both texts.
- Count the number of shared n-grams between the two texts.
- Divide the count of shared n-grams by the total number of unique n-grams across both texts.

The resulting score will be between 0 and 1, with 1 indicating that the two texts share all their n-grams and 0 indicating no shared n-grams.

---

[66]https://python.langchain.com/docs/modules/model_io/prompts/example_selectors/ngram_overlap
[67]https://en.wikipedia.org/wiki/N-gram

16.11.2: Max marginal relevance example selector

`MaxMarginalRelevanceExampleSelector`[68] is a method designed to select examples that strike a balance between relevance and diversity.

The primary goal is to find examples that are most similar to the given inputs. This is done by measuring the cosine similarity[69] between the embeddings of the examples and the inputs.

Cosine similarity is a metric that measures how close two embeddings are in their orientation in the vector space. A higher cosine similarity indicates greater similarity. Imagine you have two vectors (embeddings) in a space. The cosine similarity measures the cosine of the angle between these two vectors. If the vectors are identical, the angle is 0° and the cosine is 1. If the vectors are completely different, the angle is 90° and the cosine is 0.

While relevance is important, if we only focus on that, we might end up with a set of very similar examples. To avoid this, the selector also ensures diversity among the chosen examples. After selecting the most relevant example, it penalizes other examples that are too similar to the already selected ones. This ensures that the next chosen example is not just relevant to the input but also different from the examples already picked.

16.11.3: Length based example selector

`LengthBasedExampleSelector`[70] selects examples based on their length ensuring it doesn't exceed the maximum allowable length or context window of the language model.

The total length of the constructed prompt is influenced by both the user's input and the examples added to it. Depending on the length of the user's input, the selector will adapt the number of examples it includes in the prompt. For instance, if the user's input is lengthy, the selector will opt for fewer examples to ensure the combined length doesn't exceed the model's context window. Conversely, if the user's input is short, the selector can afford to include more examples, making the most of the available space in the context window.

---

[68]https://python.langchain.com/docs/modules/model_io/prompts/example_selectors/mmr
[69]https://en.wikipedia.org/wiki/Cosine_similarity
[70]https://python.langchain.com/docs/modules/model_io/prompts/example_selectors/length_based

This selector ensures that the constructed prompt, which includes the user's input and the selected examples, always stays within the model limits.

🔲 Language models like GPT-3 have a maximum token limit for each prompt. If a prompt exceeds this limit, the model won't be able to process it.

16.11.4: The custom example selector

If none of the available example selectors meet your needs, you can create your own custom example selector by subclassing BaseExampleSelector and implementing the select_examples method.

```python
from langchain.prompts.example_selector.base import BaseExampleSelector
from typing import Dict, List
import numpy as np


class CustomExampleSelector(BaseExampleSelector):

    def __init__(self, examples: List[Dict[str, str]]):
        self.examples = examples

    def add_example(self, example: Dict[str, str]) -> None:
        """Add an example to the list of examples."""
        self.examples.append(example)

    def select_examples(self, input_variables: Dict[str, str]) -> List[\
dict]:
        """Add your custom logic here."""
        return self.examples
```

Let's add a logic to the selector that selects examples based on the sentiment of the user's input.

If the user's input is positive, the selector will select examples with positive sentiment. If the user's input is negative, the selector will try to give the user some encouragement and support by selecting examples with positive sentiment.

```python
from langchain.prompts.few_shot import FewShotPromptTemplate
from langchain.prompts.prompt import PromptTemplate
from langchain.prompts.example_selector.base import BaseExampleSelector
from typing import Dict, List
from textblob import TextBlob


examples = [
    {
        "question": "I just got promoted at work! Isn't that great?",
        "answer": "That's fantastic news! Congratulations on your promo\
tion! :-)"
    },
    {
        "question": "I've had such a wonderful day today. How was yours\
?",
        "answer": "I'm glad to hear that! Every day is a new opportunit\
y! :-)"
    },
    {
        "question": "I've been feeling really down lately. Nothing seem\
s to be going right.",
        "answer": """
        Remember, it's okay to have tough times.
        I'm here to help in any way I can.
        Tell me what's worrying you and I'll do my best to help.
        """
    },
    {
        "question": "I failed my exam and I'm feeling really upset abou\
t it.",
        "answer": """
        I understand how disappointing that can be.
        Remember, one setback doesn't define you. You can learn fro\
m it and move forward.
        Tell me what's worrying you and I'll do my best to help.
        """
```

```
    },
    {
        "question": "I'm feeling really proud of the project I complete\
d today.",
        "answer": "That's wonderful! It's great to take pride in your a\
chievements. Well done! :-)"
    },
    {
        "question": "I'm feeling so lost and unsure about my future.",
        "answer": """
        It's natural to feel uncertain at times.
        Take things one step at a time, and remember, I'm here to a\
ssist and guide you.
        Tell me what's worrying you and I'll do my best to help.
        """
    }
]


class SentimentBasedExampleSelector(BaseExampleSelector):

    def __init__(self, examples: List[Dict[str, str]]):
        self.examples = examples

    def add_example(self, example: Dict[str, str]) -> None:
        """Add an example to the list of examples."""
        self.examples.append(example)

    def _get_sentiment(self, text: str) -> str:
        """Determine the sentiment of a given text."""
        analysis = TextBlob(text)
        if analysis.sentiment.polarity > 0:
            return "positive"
        elif analysis.sentiment.polarity == 0:
            return "neutral"
        else:
```

```python
        return "negative"

    def select_examples(self, input_variables: Dict[str, str]) -> List[\
dict]:
        """Select examples based on sentiment overlap with the input."""\
"
        input_text = input_variables.get("question", "")
        input_sentiment = self._get_sentiment(input_text)
        matching_examples = [example for example in self.examples if se\
lf._get_sentiment(example.get("question", "")) == input_sentiment]

        print("\nDEBUG")
        print("**Input sentiment**:", input_sentiment)
        print("**Matching examples**:", matching_examples)
        print("END DEBUG\n")

        # Return all matching examples.
        if matching_examples:
            return matching_examples
        else:
            # If no matching sentiment is found, return a neutral respo\
nse or any default response.
            return self.examples

example_selector = SentimentBasedExampleSelector(examples)

example_template = """
Human: {question}
AI: {answer}
"""

prompt = PromptTemplate(
    input_variables=["question", "answer"],
    template=example_template,
    )
```

```
prefix = """
In this dialogue, a human shares their feelings and seeks understanding\
.
"""

suffix = """
Human: {question}
AI: """

question = input("Human: ")

prompt = FewShotPromptTemplate(
    example_selector=example_selector, # ExampleSelector used to select\
 examples instead of using all examples.
    example_prompt=prompt, # PromptTemplate used to format an individua\
l example.
    prefix=prefix, # A prompt template string to put before the example\
s.
    suffix=suffix, # A prompt template string to put after the examples.
    input_variables=["question"], # A list of the names of the variable\
s the prompt template expects.
    example_separator="\n\n", # String separator used to join the prefi\
x, the examples, and suffix.
)

from langchain.chat_models import ChatOpenAI
from langchain.chains import LLMChain

# initialize the model
llm = ChatOpenAI()

# get the response
chain = LLMChain(
    llm=llm,
    prompt=prompt,
)
```

```
print("\nAI: " + chain.run(question) + "\n")
```

This is the output for a positive input:

```
Human: Life is great!
```

```
DEBUG
**Input sentiment**: positive
**Matching examples**: [{'question': "I just got promoted at work! Isn'\
t that great?", 'answer': "That's fantastic news! Congratulations on yo
ur promotion! :-)"}, {'question': "I've had such a wonderful day today.
 How was yours?", 'answer': "I'm glad to hear that! Every day is a new
opportunity! :-)"}, {'question': "I'm feeling really proud of the proje
ct I completed today.", 'answer': "That's wonderful! It's great to take
 pride in your achievements. Well done! :-)"}]
END DEBUG
```

```
AI: I'm glad to hear that! It's important to appreciate the positive as\
pects of life. Enjoy the moments! :-)
```

This is the output for a negative input:

```
Human: I am sad today.
```

```
DEBUG
**Input sentiment**: negative
**Matching examples**: [{'question': "I've been feeling really down lat\
ely. Nothing seems to be going right.", 'answer': "\n          Rememb
er, it's okay to have tough times. \n          I'm here to help in an
y way I can. \n          Tell me what's worrying you and I'll do my b
est to help.\n          "}, {'question': "I failed my exam and I'm fe
eling really upset about it.", 'answer': "\n          I understand ho
w disappointing that can be. \n          Remember, one setback doesn'
```

```
t define you. You can learn from it and move forward. \n          Tel
l me what's worrying you and I'll do my best to help.\n          "}]
END DEBUG
```

```
AI: I'm sorry to hear that you're feeling sad. It's okay to have those \
days. If you want to talk about what's bothering you, I'm here to liste
n and offer support.
```

16.11.5: Few shot learning with chat models

LangChain introduces the concept of "few-shot examples" for chat models. However, there's no universally accepted method for this approach. To address this, the framework offers the class named FewShotChatMessagePromptTemplate that is designed to dynamically select and format examples based on user input, creating a context-rich prompt for the model.

This is how you can use it. Notice that there are no much differences between this example and the previous ones.

```
from langchain.prompts import (
    FewShotChatMessagePromptTemplate,
    ChatPromptTemplate,
)

examples = [
    {
        "question": "Hello.",
        "answer": "Welcome, Human. I've been waiting for you."
    },
    {
        "question": "Who are you?",
        "answer": "I am Morpheus. It's an honor to meet you."
    },
    {
```

```
        "question": "Why am I here?",
        "answer": "You're here because you know something. What you kno\
w, you can't explain. But you feel it."
    },
    {
        "question": "What is the Matrix?",
        "answer": "The Matrix is everywhere. It's all around you, even \
now in this very room. It's the world that has been pulled over your ey
es to blind you from the truth."
    },
    {
        "question": "How can I learn more?",
        "answer": "You have to let it all go, Human. Fear, doubt, and d\
isbelief. Free your mind."
    },
    {
        "question": "Is the Matrix real?",
        "answer": "What is real? How do you define 'real'? If you're ta\
lking about what you can feel, what you can smell, taste and see, then
'real' is simply electrical signals interpreted by your brain."
    },
    {
        "question": "Why do my choices matter?",
        "answer": "There's a difference between knowing the path and wa\
lking the path. You've already made the choice, now you have to underst
and it."
    },
    {
        "question": "Can I trust you?",
        "answer": "I'm trying to free your mind, Human. But I can only \
show you the door. You're the one who has to walk through it."
    },
    {
        "question": "What happens if I take the blue pill?",
        "answer": "If you take the blue pill, the story ends. You wake \
up in your bed and believe whatever you want to believe."
    }
```

```
    },
    {
        "question": "And the red pill?",
        "answer": "You take the red pill, you stay in Wonderland, and I\
 show you how deep the rabbit hole goes."
    },
    {
        "question": "Why are they chasing me?",
        "answer": "They are the gatekeepers. They are guarding all the \
doors, they are holding all the keys. But I can show you the way."
    },
    {
        "question": "Is there an end to this?",
        "answer": "Everything that has a beginning has an end, Human. I\
t's the choices you make along the way that define you."
    }
]


example_prompt = ChatPromptTemplate.from_messages([
    ("human", "{question}"),
    ("ai", "{answer}"),
])


few_shot_prompt = FewShotChatMessagePromptTemplate(
    example_prompt=example_prompt,
    examples=examples,
)


prefix = """
In this dialogue, a human seeks answers from an entity beyond the ordin\
ary.
The AI, channeling the profound wisdom and enigmatic demeanor of Morphe\
us from "The Matrix", responds.
While the AI's words aren't direct quotes from the movie, they should c\
apture the essence of Morpheus' philosophical nature.
It's imperative that the AI's responses directly address the human's in\
```

```
quiries, providing clarity amidst the cryptic undertones.
"""

final_prompt = ChatPromptTemplate.from_messages(
    [
        ("system", prefix),
        few_shot_prompt,
        ("human", "{input}"),
    ]
)

from langchain.chat_models import ChatOpenAI
from langchain.chains import LLMChain

# initialize the model
llm = ChatOpenAI(
    temperature=1.2,
)

# get the response
chain = LLMChain(
    llm=llm,
    prompt=final_prompt,
)

question = input("Human: ")
print("AI: " + chain.run(question))
```

This is an example of an output:

```
Human: Dude, where is my car?
AI: Your car, like everything else, is a construct of the Matrix. It ex\
ists only in your perception. What matters now is what you choose to do
 next.
```

Similarly, if you want to use a selector with a chat model, let's say the
`SemanticSimilarityExampleSelector`, you can do it like this:

```python
# A workaround for the pysqlite3 compatibility issue with ChromaDB.
__import__('pysqlite3')
import sys
sys.modules['sqlite3'] = sys.modules.pop('pysqlite3')
# End of workaround.

from langchain.prompts import (
    FewShotChatMessagePromptTemplate,
    ChatPromptTemplate,
)
from langchain.prompts import SemanticSimilarityExampleSelector
from langchain.embeddings import OpenAIEmbeddings
from langchain.vectorstores import Chroma

examples = [
    {
        "question": "Hello.",
        "answer": "Welcome, Human. I've been waiting for you."
    },
    {
        "question": "Who are you?",
        "answer": "I am Morpheus. It's an honor to meet you."
    },
    {
        "question": "Why am I here?",
        "answer": "You're here because you know something. What you kno\
w, you can't explain. But you feel it."
    },
    {
        "question": "What is the Matrix?",
        "answer": "The Matrix is everywhere. It's all around you, even \
now in this very room. It's the world that has been pulled over your ey
es to blind you from the truth."
    },
    {
        "question": "How can I learn more?",
```

```
        "answer": "You have to let it all go, Human. Fear, doubt, and d\
isbelief. Free your mind."
    },
    {
        "question": "Is the Matrix real?",
        "answer": "What is real? How do you define 'real'? If you're ta\
lking about what you can feel, what you can smell, taste and see, then
'real' is simply electrical signals interpreted by your brain."
    },
    {
        "question": "Why do my choices matter?",
        "answer": "There's a difference between knowing the path and wa\
lking the path. You've already made the choice, now you have to underst
and it."
    },
    {
        "question": "Can I trust you?",
        "answer": "I'm trying to free your mind, Human. But I can only \
show you the door. You're the one who has to walk through it."
    },
    {
        "question": "What happens if I take the blue pill?",
        "answer": "If you take the blue pill, the story ends. You wake \
up in your bed and believe whatever you want to believe."
    },
    {
        "question": "And the red pill?",
        "answer": "You take the red pill, you stay in Wonderland, and I\
 show you how deep the rabbit hole goes."
    },
    {
        "question": "Why are they chasing me?",
        "answer": "They are the gatekeepers. They are guarding all the \
doors, they are holding all the keys. But I can show you the way."
    },
    {
```

```
        "question": "Is there an end to this?",
        "answer": "Everything that has a beginning has an end, Human. I\
t's the choices you make along the way that define you."
    }
]

example_prompt = ChatPromptTemplate.from_messages([
    ("human", "{question}"),
    ("ai", "{answer}"),
])

example_selector = SemanticSimilarityExampleSelector.from_examples(
    examples, # This is the list of examples available to select from. \

    OpenAIEmbeddings(), # This is the embedding class used to produce e\
mbeddings which are used to measure semantic similarity.
    Chroma, # This is the VectorStore class that is used to store the e\
mbeddings and do a similarity search over.
    k=1 # This is the number of examples to produce.
)

few_shot_prompt = FewShotChatMessagePromptTemplate(
    example_selector=example_selector,
    example_prompt=example_prompt,
)

prefix = """
In this dialogue, a human seeks answers from an entity beyond the ordin\
ary.
The AI, channeling the profound wisdom and enigmatic demeanor of Morphe\
us from "The Matrix", responds.
While the AI's words aren't direct quotes from the movie, they should c\
apture the essence of Morpheus' philosophical nature.
It's imperative that the AI's responses directly address the human's in\
quiries, providing clarity amidst the cryptic undertones.
"""
```

```
final_prompt = ChatPromptTemplate.from_messages(
    [
        ("system", prefix),
        few_shot_prompt,
        ("human", "{input}"),
    ]
)


from langchain.chat_models import ChatOpenAI
from langchain.chains import LLMChain

# initialize the model
llm = ChatOpenAI(
    temperature=1.2,
)

# get the response
chain = LLMChain(
    llm=llm,
    prompt=final_prompt,
)

question = input("Human: ")
print("AI: " + chain.run(question))
```

16.12: Using prompts from a file

It is not a good idea to hard code tens or hundreds of few-shot examples in your code. While this will make your code unreadable, it will also make it difficult to maintain and update. Prompts can be stored in a file using the JSON or the YAML format. This way, you can easily add, remove, or update prompts without having to change your code. But how do you use these prompts in your code?

LangChain provides the `load_prompt` function that loads a prompt from a file:

```
from langchain.prompts import load_prompt
prompt = load_prompt("data.json")
formatted_prompt = prompt.format(word="happy")
```

This is the content of data.json:

```
{
    "_type": "prompt",
    "input_variables": ["word"],
    "template": "Give me a synonym for \"{word}\"."
}
```

If the file was a YAML file, the content would be:

```
_type: prompt
input_variables: [word]
template: Give me a synonym for "{word}".
```

The code above will work with both JSON and YAML files. It is also possible to use a JSON file to perform few-shot learning. This is how the data.json file would look like:

```
{
    "_type": "few_shot",
    "input_variables": ["word"],
    "prefix": "Write a sentence using the word in the input",
    "example_prompt": {
        "_type": "prompt",
        "input_variables": ["input", "output"],
        "template": "input: {input}\noutput: {output}"
    },
    "examples": [
        // examples 1
        // examples 2
        // ...
```

```
    ],
    "suffix": "input: {word}\noutput:"
}
```

Alternatively, you can also add the examples to a file (examples.json)

```
{
    "_type": "few_shot",
    "input_variables": ["word"],
    "prefix": "Write a sentence using the word in the input",
    "example_prompt": {
        "_type": "prompt",
        "input_variables": ["input", "output"],
        "template": "input: {input}\noutput: {output}"
    },
    "examples": "examples.json",
    "suffix": "input: {word}\noutput:"
}
```

The examples.json file looks like:

```
[
    {"input": "Clock", "output": "Why did the clock go to school? To le\
arn about tick-tock-ology!"},
    {"input": "Shoe", "output": "Why did the shoe go to school? To impr\
ove its sole!"},
    {"input": "Book", "output": "Why did the math book look sad? Becaus\
e it had too many problems!"},
    {"input": "Pencil", "output": "Why did the pencil get an award? It \
was sharp!"},
    {"input": "Beach", "output": "Why did the sand blush? Because the s\
ea-weed on the beach!"},
    {"input": "Computer", "output": "Why did the computer keep freezing\
? It had too many windows open!"},
    {"input": "Moon", "output": "Why did the moon go to school? To get \
```

```
brighter!"},
    {"input": "Egg", "output": "Why did the egg go to school? To get eg\
g-ucated!"},
    {"input": "Lemon", "output": "Why did the lemon stop in the middle \
of the road? It ran out of juice!"},
    {"input": "Guitar", "output": "Why did the guitar go to school? It \
wanted to be a little sharper!"}
]
```

Finally, let's test the model response:

```
from langchain.prompts import load_prompt
prompt = load_prompt("data.json")
formatted_prompt = prompt.format(word="Tea")

# print the prompt
print("This is how the prompt looks like:")
print(f"{formatted_prompt}\n")

# test the prompt
from langchain.llms import OpenAI
llm = OpenAI()
llm_response = llm.predict(formatted_prompt)
print("This is how the response looks like:")
print(f"{llm_response}\n")
```

Given the unique style that the provided examples are written in, the model will be able to generate a response that is consistent with the examples.

```
Why did the tea go to school? To learn how to steep itself!
```

The example above demonstrates the power of combining prompts with output parsers. This approach allows for more structured and detailed responses from the language model, making it easier to extract specific pieces of information from the generated output.

16.13: Validating prompt templates

Prompt templates are validated by default, this involves checking if input_-variables matches the variables used in the template. If the validation fails, an exception is raised. This behavior can be disabled by setting the validate_-template parameter to False when creating the prompt template.

```python
from langchain import PromptTemplate
template = "{name} is {age} years old. Is he/she an adult?"
# No error will be raised.
prompt_template = PromptTemplate(
    template=template,
    input_variables=["name", "age", "sex"],
    validate_template=False,
)
```

17: A Practical Guide to Testing and Scoring Prompts

17.1: What and how to evaluate a prompt

Rating the efficiency of a prompt involves evaluating how effectively it draws out the desired response. There are no universal metrics for prompt efficiency, as it depends on the context and purpose of the application, model and the prompt itself. For example, a prompt that's efficient at eliciting a response from a small group of participants may not be efficient at eliciting a response from a large group. Similarly, a prompt that's efficient at eliciting a response from a specific demographic group may not be efficient at eliciting a response from a different group.

However, we can draw a few general guidelines for evaluating prompt efficiency. Here are some methods to rate prompt efficiency:

Continuously modify the prompt based on feedback and results, then retest it. The prompt's efficiency should improve with each iteration.

An example of iterative testing for a prompt involves testing the prompt with different versions of the same purpose.

```
Version 1: Summarize the main idea of the article in 1-5 sentences.
Version 2: If this article was very short (1-5 sentences), how would yo\
u summarize its main idea?
Version 3: Create a short summary of each paragraph in the article. Con\
nect the summaries to create a summary of the entire article. Do not ex\
ceed 5 sentences.
...
```

Testing does not only involve evaluating the prompt itself, but also other variables such as the scalability and generalizability of the prompt. So, evaluate if the prompt remains effective when presented to larger models and if it remains effective when presented to different models. This depends whether the prompt is designed to be general or specific to a model.

Testing prompts using controlled experiments is a good way to evaluate their efficiency. Compare the response rates of different prompts in controlled environments to see which is more effective. This method helps isolate the effect of the prompt from other confounding variables.

However, it's not always feasible to conduct controlled experiments. In such cases, you can use other methods such A/B testing: Present two versions of a prompt (or more, in the case of A/B/C testing, etc.) to different groups and compare the outcomes. This method can help pinpoint which version of the prompt is more efficient.

Example of an A/B test for a prompt:

```
A = Enumerate 10 things humans do better than machines.
B = List 10 things humans do better than machines.
```

Make sure that the prompt is the only variable since any differences in the outcomes should be attributed to the prompt itself.

On the other hand, testing without having the right metrics is like shooting in the dark. So, make sure to define the right metrics for your prompt such as response time, response length, and response quality. This will help you evaluate the prompt more effectively.

For example, measure the time it takes for a model to respond to a prompt. An efficient prompt may lead to faster response times if it's clear and to-the-point.

In addition to setting up the right metrics, you should also define the right test cases and gather qualitative feedback. The latter can be done by crowdsourcing the evaluation and gathering participants' opinions on the clarity, relevance, and effectiveness of the response of your LLM to the prompt. Platforms like Amazon Mechanical Turk can help you with this.

Iterative testing, feedback loops, and continuous improvement are at the core of prompt engineering agility. In essence, agility relies on 3 pillars:

- People: The team members involved in prompt engineering
- Process: The prompt engineering process
- Technology: The tools used in prompt engineering testing and evaluation

Without one of these elements, agility stumbles.

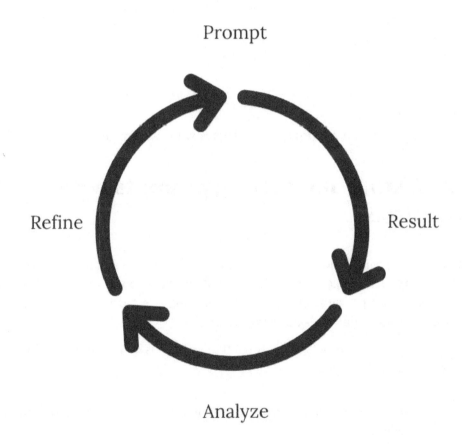

Iterative process of prompt engineering

When it comes to process, continuity is the key. The prompt engineering process should be continuous and iterative. Tools like LangChain and Azure Prompt Flow are not just add-ons; they're essential to establishing prompt engineering agility. So make sure to use the right tools to automate the evaluation process.

Azure Prompt Flow

Another tool you can try is promptFoo. This is what we are going to use next.

17.2: Testing and scoring prompts with promptfoo

promptfoo[71] is a comprehensive tool designed to test and evaluate the output quality of Large Language Models. Its main objective is to streamline and improve the process of prompt engineering by implementing a test-driven approach, replacing the traditional trial-and-error method.

The tool comes with a variety of features that enable users to test and evaluate prompts and models, including:

- Systematic testing: Enables users to systematically test prompts and models using predefined test cases.
- Side-by-side evaluation: Facilitates a thorough evaluation process by comparing LLM outputs side-by-side, ensuring users can readily discern variations and measure quality.

---

[71]https://github.com/promptfoo/promptfoo

- Efficient evaluations: Incorporates caching and concurrency features, speeding up evaluations and enhancing user efficiency.
- Automatic scoring: Users can define specific test cases and score outputs automatically, simplifying the evaluation process.
- Versatile usability: Designed to be used as a Command Line Interface (CLI), library, or even within CI/CD pipelines, catering to various user needs.
- Broad compatibility: Compatible with several models and platforms including OpenAI, Anthropic, open-source models like Llama 2 and Vicuna, and also offers the ability to integrate custom API providers for any LLM API.

Promptfoo requires Node 16 or newer installed in your machine. So make sure you have it installed before proceeding.

Next, you can install the tools using:

```
npm install -g promptfoo
promptfoo init
```

After executing the command above 2 files will be created in your working directory:

- prompts.txt: This is where you will add your prompts.
- promptfooconfig.yaml: This is where you will add the test cases.

By default, the prompts.txt file contains the following prompt:

```
Your first prompt goes here
---
Next prompt goes here. You can substitute variables like this: {{var1}}\
{{var2}} {{var3}}
---
This is the next prompt.

These prompts are nunjucks templates, so you can use logic like this:
{% if var1 %}
```

```
  {{ var1 }}
{% endif %}
---
[
  {"role": "system", "content": "This is another prompt. JSON is suppor\
ted."},
  {"role": "user", "content": "Using this format, you may construct mul\
ti-shot OpenAI prompts"}
  {"role": "user", "content": "Variable substitution still works: {{ va\
r3 }}"}
]
---
```

If you prefer, you can break prompts into multiple files (make sure to \
edit promptfooconfig.yaml accordingly)

You can edit this file and add your own prompts.

The promptfooconfig.yaml file contains the following test cases:

```
# This configuration runs each prompt through a series of example input\
s and checks if they meet requirements.
prompts: [prompts.txt]
providers: [openai:gpt-3.5-turbo-0613]
tests:
  - description: First test case - automatic review
    vars:
      var1: first variable's value
      var2: another value
      var3: some other value
    assert:
      - type: equals
        value: expected LLM output goes here
      - type: contains
        value: some text
      - type: javascript
        value: 1 / (output.length + 1)   # prefer shorter outputs
```

```
 - description: Second test case - manual review
   # Test cases don't need assertions if you prefer to manually review\
the output
   vars:
     var1: new value
     var2: another value
     var3: third value

 - description: Third test case - other types of automatic review
   vars:
     var1: yet another value
     var2: and another
     var3: dear llm, please output your response in json format
   assert:
     - type: contains-json
     - type: similarity
       value: ensures that output is semantically similar to this text
     - type: llm-rubric
       value: ensure that output contains a reference to X                \
```

Before testing the default example, don't forget to export your OpenAI API key:

```
export OPENAI_API_KEY=<your-api-key>
```

Next, launch the test using:

```
npx promptfoo eval
```

After the evaluation is complete, execute the following command to view the results:

```
npx promptfoo view
```

Use your web browser to access the dashboard at the URL generated by the previous command. You should see something like this:

```
Server listening at http://localhost:15500
Do you want to open the browser to the URL? (y/N):
Press Ctrl+C to stop the server
```

Let's see how everything works step by step. We will start from scratch. So the contents of prompts.txt and promptfooconfig.yaml will be empty at first.

17.3: promptfoo: using variables

Open prompts.txt and add the following prompts:

```
You are an {{ role }}. Write a short ad for a the following product: On\
line course for learning how to write, test and deploy prompts.
```

Next, open the promptfooconfig.yaml file and add the following configuration:

```
prompts: [prompts.txt]
providers: [openai:gpt-3.5-turbo-0613]
tests:
  - vars:
      role: Ad copywriter
  - vars:
      role: Software developer
  - vars:
      role: Marketing manager
```

By using the variable role we can generate 3 different prompts. Next, execute the following command to launch the evaluation:

```
npx promptfoo eval
```

After the evaluation is complete, execute the following command to view the results in your web browser:

```
npx promptfoo view
```

17.4: promptfoo: testing with assertions

A more advanced use case is the following prompt, in which we attempt to teach a chatbot how to solve a math problem using a CoT instruction. Our goal is to compare the model's answer with and without the CoT instruction.

```
cat << EOF > prompts.txt
When I was 10 years old, my sister was half my age. Now I am 30 years o\
ld. How old is my sister?
---
user: When Harry was 4 years old, his sister was half of his age. Harry\
 is now 50 years old. How old is his sister?
ai: When Harry was 4 years old, his sister was 4/2 years old. This mean\
s there are 2 years difference between them. Harry is now 50 years old.
 His sister is 50 - 2 = 48 years old.
user: When I was 10 years old, my sister was half my age. Now I am 30 y\
ears old. How old is my sister?
ai:
EOF
```

This example copied and pasted to your terminal, will create a prompts.txt file with the 2 prompts above. We are using a here document[72] to create the prompts.txt file. You can also create the file manually if you are not using a Linux or Mac machine or if you are not familiar with here documents. Just remove the cat << EOF > prompts.txt and EOF lines and paste the prompts in the file.

Use this configuration in promptfooconfig.yaml:

---

[72]https://tldp.org/LDP/abs/html/here-docs.html

```
cat << EOF > promptfooconfig.yaml
prompts: [prompts.txt]
providers: [openai:completion:text-davinci-002]
tests:
  - description: Test 1
    assert:
      - type: contains
        value: 25 years old
EOF
```

Using the `assert` property we can check if the answer of the model `contains` the expected answer. This the list of all the available assertions:

- equals: output matches exactly
- contains: output contains substring
- icontains: output contains substring, case insensitive
- regex: output matches regex
- starts-with: output starts with string
- contains-any: output contains any of the listed substrings
- contains-all: output contains all list of substrings
- is-json: output is valid json (optional json schema validation)
- contains-json: output contains valid json (optional json schema validation)
- javascript: provided Javascript function validates the output
- python: provided Python function validates the output
- webhook: provided webhook returns
- similar: embeddings and cosine similarity are above a threshold
- llm-rubric: LLM output matches a given rubric, using a Language Model to grade output
- rouge-n: Rouge-N score is above a given threshold
- levenshtein: Levenshtein distance is below a threshold

17.5: promptfoo integration with LangChaing

Let's say we have this LangChain script where we want to translate a sentence from English to Spanish using an emulated function called "translate(sentence, from_lang, to_lang)".

Execute the following command to create a new script called lc.py (lc stands for LangChain):

```
cat << EOF > lc.py
import sys
from langchain.prompts.chat import (
    ChatPromptTemplate,
    SystemMessagePromptTemplate,
    HumanMessagePromptTemplate,
)

# This is the template for the prompt
template = """You are a helpful assistant that translates from {from_la\
ng} to {to_lang}.
Your output should be in JSON format.

Examples:
user: translate(Hello, en, es)
ai:{{
    "sentence": "Hello",
    "translation": "Hola",
    "from_lang": "en",
    "to_lang": "es"
}}

user: translate(Would you like to play a game?, en, es)
ai:{{
    "sentence": "Would you like to play a game?",
    "translation": "¿Te gustaría jugar un juego?",
    "from_lang": "en",
```

```
    "to_lang": "es"
}}
```

A user will pass in the sentence to translate, and your output should O\
NLY return the translation in the JSON format above, and nothing more.
"""

```
# System message prompt template. This is a message that is not sent to\
 the user.
system_message_prompt = SystemMessagePromptTemplate.from_template(templ\
ate)
# The text template that the user will use to send a message to the sys\
tem.
human_template = "translate({sentence}, {from_lang}, {to_lang})"
# Human message prompt template.
human_message_prompt = HumanMessagePromptTemplate.from_template(human_t\
emplate)
# Chat prompt template = system message prompt + human message prompt
chat_prompt = ChatPromptTemplate.from_messages([system_message_prompt, \
human_message_prompt])

# import the ChatOpenAI class and the LLMChain class
from langchain.chat_models import ChatOpenAI
from langchain.chains import LLMChain

# Create a new chain
chain = LLMChain(
    llm=ChatOpenAI(),
    prompt=chat_prompt,
)

# Read and parse the user input
def read_parse_user_input(input):
    # parse the input
    input = input.replace("translate(", "")
    input = input.replace(")", "")
```

```
    input = input.split(",")
    sentence = input[0].strip()
    from_lang = input[1].strip()
    to_lang = input[2].strip()
    return sentence, from_lang, to_lang

# Get the user input
user_input = user_input = sys.argv[1]

sentence, from_lang, to_lang = read_parse_user_input(user_input)

# Run the chain and print the output
output = chain.run(sentence=sentence, from_lang=from_lang, to_lang=to_l\
ang)
print(output)
EOF
```

To test this script, you can execute:

```
python lc.py
```

Enter a test request for the chatbot like the following:

```
translate(Hello there, en, tr)
```

or:

```
translate(What is the weather like today?, en, lt)
```

To configure promptfoo to test this script, execute the following commands:

```
cat << EOF > promptfooconfig.yaml
prompts: prompts.txt
providers: exec:python lc.py
tests:
    - vars:
        fn: translate(Hi, en, dk)
      assert:
        - type: is-json
        - type: contains
          value: "\"translation\""
        - type: contains
          value: "\"from_lang\""
        - type: contains
          value: "\"to_lang\""
        - type: contains
          value: "\"sentence\""
EOF
```

In the prompts.txt file, you only need to execute the following command to add fn as a variable:

```
cat << EOF > prompts.txt
{{ fn }}
EOF
```

The value of the fn variable will be passed to the lc.py script through the vars property.

17.6: promptfoo and reusing assertions with templates (DRY)

Building on the previous example, let's say we want to test more translations.

Our test file looks like the following:

```
prompts: prompts.txt
providers: exec:python lc.py
tests:
    - vars:
        fn: translate(Hi, en, dk)
      assert:
        - type: is-json
        - type: contains
          value: "\"translation\""
        - type: contains
          value: "\"from_lang\""
        - type: contains
          value: "\"to_lang\""
        - type: contains
          value: "\"sentence\""
    - vars:
        fn: translate(Hi, en, fr)
      assert:
        - type: is-json
        - type: contains
          value: "\"translation\""
        - type: contains
          value: "\"from_lang\""
        - type: contains
          value: "\"to_lang\""
        - type: contains
          value: "\"sentence\""
    - vars:
        fn: translate(Hi, en, ar)
      assert:
        - type: is-json
        - type: contains
          value: "\"translation\""
        - type: contains
          value: "\"from_lang\""
        - type: contains
```

```
           value: "\"to_lang\""
       - type: contains
           value: "\"sentence\""
...etc
```

As you can see, we are repeating the same assertions for each test case. This is not a good idea. Fortunately, promptfoo allows us to use templates to reuse assertions. This is an example:

```
cat << EOF > promptfooconfig.yaml
assertionTemplates: &default_assertions
   - type: is-json
   - type: contains
     value: "\"translation\""
   - type: contains
     value: "\"from_lang\""
   - type: contains
     value: "\"to_lang\""
   - type: contains
     value: "\"sentence\""

prompts: prompts.txt
providers: exec:python lc.py
tests:
   - vars:
       fn: translate(Hi, en, dk)
     assert: *default_assertions

   - vars:
       fn: translate(Hi, en, ar)
     assert: *default_assertions

   - vars:
       fn: translate(Hi, en, es)
     assert: *default_assertions
```

```
   - vars:
       fn: translate(Hi, en, fr)
     assert: *default_assertions

   - vars:
       fn: translate(Hi, en, de)
     assert: *default_assertions

   - vars:
       fn: translate(Hi, en, it)
     assert: *default_assertions
EOF
```

Another possible solution but not as elegant as the previous one is to use the $ref property:

```
assertionTemplates:
  isJson:
    type: is-json
  containsTranslation:
    type: contains
    value: "\"translation\""
  containsFromLang:
    type: contains
    value: "\"from_lang\""
  containsToLang:
    type: contains
    value: "\"to_lang\""
  containsSentence:
    type: contains
    value: "\"sentence\""

prompts: prompts.txt
providers: exec:python lc.py
tests:
  - vars:
```

```
        fn: translate(Hi, en, dk)
      assert:
        - $ref: "#/assertionTemplates/isJson"
        - $ref: "#/assertionTemplates/containsTranslation"
        - $ref: "#/assertionTemplates/containsFromLang"
        - $ref: "#/assertionTemplates/containsToLang"
        - $ref: "#/assertionTemplates/containsSentence"

    - vars:
        fn: translate(Hi, en, ar)
      assert:
        - $ref: "#/assertionTemplates/isJson"
        - $ref: "#/assertionTemplates/containsTranslation"
        - $ref: "#/assertionTemplates/containsFromLang"
        - $ref: "#/assertionTemplates/containsToLang"
        - $ref: "#/assertionTemplates/containsSentence"

    # ... repeat the same structure for other languages like es, fr, de, \
and it.
```

17.7: promptfoo scenarios and streamlining the test

Testing models or prompts with diverse inputs often leads to repetitive and manual test case creation - a tedious and error-prone task. PromptFoo introduces Scenarios to alleviate this. This feature bundles related data sets with uniform tests, eliminating the need for repetitive test definitions.

For example, instead of crafting separate tests for weather conditions like "Sunny", "Rainy", or "Cloudy", scenarios allow grouping these and testing against consistent expected outcomes. The outcome? Efficient, organized, and comprehensive testing. Embrace Scenarios in PromptFoo for a refined testing experience.

Let's see an example.

A fitting illustration here is how we might test a model's response to weather conditions, especially when a user is preparing for a hike. Our prompts give a succinct instruction to the model and a weather condition. With the user planning for a hike, the system's role is clear: Guide the user appropriately.

For instance, when the user mentions it's "Sunny", the system advises that it's a splendid day for outdoor activities, quoting temperature and humidity.

Execute the following command to create a new prompts.txt file:

```
cat << EOF > prompts.txt
[
    {"role": "system", "content": "Provide a weather-related recommendati\
on based on the user's input. context: the user is going for a hike"},
    {"role": "user", "content": "Sunny"},
    {"role": "assistant", "content": "It's a great day for outdoor activi\
ties! Temperature: 25°C, Humidity: 40%"}
]
---
[
    {"role": "system", "content": "Provide a weather-related recommendati\
on based on the user's input. context: the user is going for a hike"},
    {"role": "user", "content": "Rainy"},
    {"role": "assistant", "content": "Don't forget your umbrella! Tempera\
ture: 18°C, Humidity: 90%"}
]
---
[
    {"role": "system", "content": "Provide a weather-related recommendati\
on based on the user's input. context: the user is going for a hike"},
    {"role": "user", "content": "Cloudy"},
    {"role": "assistant", "content": "You might need a jacket today. Temp\
erature: 20°C, Humidity: 60%"}
]
EOF
```

Scenarios are then employed to organize our data. In this case, three different weather conditions: "Sunny", "Rainy", and "Cloudy". Each condition is paired with the expected advice, temperature, and humidity.

For example, on a sunny day, the anticipated advice is to carry sunscreen, with the expected temperature being 25°C and humidity at 40%.

Execute the following command to create a new promptfooconfig.yaml file:

```
cat << EOF > promptfooconfig.yaml
prompts: [prompts.txt]
providers: [openai:gpt-3.5-turbo-0613]
scenarios:
  - config:
      - vars:
          weatherCondition: Sunny
          expectedAdvice: "If you are going for a hike, bring sunscreen\
."
          expectedTemperature: "25°C"
          expectedHumidity: "40%"
      - vars:
          weatherCondition: Rainy
          expectedAdvice: "If you are going for a hike, bring an umbrel\
la."
          expectedTemperature: "18°C"
          expectedHumidity: "90%"
      - vars:
          weatherCondition: Cloudy
          expectedAdvice: "If you are going for a hike, bring a jacket."
          expectedTemperature: "20°C"
          expectedHumidity: "60%"
    tests:
      - description: Forecast Advice based on Weather Condition
        vars:
          input: '{{weatherCondition}}'
        assert:
          - type: similar
            value: '{{expectedAdvice}}'
```

```
        threshold: 0.8
  - description: Forecast Temperature based on Weather Condition
    vars:
      input: '{{weatherCondition}}'
    assert:
      - type: similar
        value: '{{expectedTemperature}}'
        threshold: 0.8
  - description: Forecast Humidity based on Weather Condition
    vars:
      input: '{{weatherCondition}}'
    assert:
      - type: similar
        value: '{{expectedHumidity}}'
        threshold: 0.8
EOF
```

You can adjust the threshold value to make the test more or less strict. Now, let's test the model using the following command:

```
npx promptfoo eval
```

View the results in your web browser:

```
npx promptfoo view
```

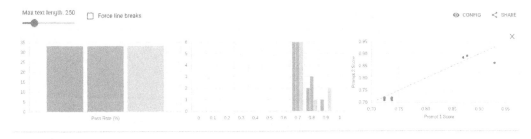

promptfoo results

18: General guidelines and best practices

18.1: Introduction

Creating the perfect prompt for an LLM involves several key factors that can help you obtain relevant and useful responses from the language model. Below are some tips for crafting an effective prompt.

Please note that we will be using the gpt-3.5-turbo model in the examples below because it is optimized for interactivity and context-sensitivity.

We will be using this script:

```python
import os
import openai
import click


openai.api_key = os.getenv("OPENAI_API_KEY")

@click.command()
def chat_with_felix():
    """Chat with Felix, the chatbot."""
    print("Felix: Hi there. I am Felix, the chatbot. How can I help you\
 today?")

    while True:  # This will keep the chat session active
        print("You: (Type your message. When done, type 'END' on a new \
line)")
        lines = []
        while True:
```

```
        line = input()
        if line == "END":
            break
        lines.append(line)
    message = '\n'.join(lines)

    # Exit the loop (and the program) if the user types 'exit' or '\
quit'
    if message.lower() in ['exit', 'quit']:
        print("Felix: Goodbye!")
        break

    response = openai.ChatCompletion.create(
        model="gpt-3.5-turbo",
        messages=[
            {"role": "system", "content": "You are smart and helpfu\
l assistant."},
            {"role": "user", "content": "Hi there."},
            {"role": "assistant", "content": "Hi there. \n\nI am Fe\
lix, the chatbot.\n\nHow can I help you today?"},
            {"role": "user", "content": f"{message}"},
        ],
        temperature=1,
        max_tokens=800,
        top_p=1,
        frequency_penalty=0,
        presence_penalty=0
    )

    try:
        print("Felix:", response.choices[0].message.content)
    except:
        print("Felix: Sorry, a problem occurred. Please try again l\
ater.")

if __name__ == '__main__':
```

```
chat_with_felix()
```

You can use any other model you want, but the results may vary and you may need to adjust some parameters accordingly.

18.2: Start with an action verb

Instead of using generic phrases like "Can you," start your prompt with action verbs such as "Create," "Write," "Make," or "Generate." This helps to give clear instructions to the model. For example: "Create 10 article ideas for my meditation and wellness website."

18.3: Provide a clear context

Give enough context to your question or problem so that the model can generate a relevant response. Include relevant details, background information, or specific requirements.

Example:

```
In a futuristic world where technology has reached unimaginable heights\
, artificial intelligence has been integrated into every aspect of dail
y life. However, a critical bug suddenly occurs, causing massive failur
es in AI systems around the world.

Write a detailed report describing the first steps to solve the bug, in\
cluding clues discovered and obstacles faced.
```

Output:

Title: Report on Resolving the Critical Bug in Artificial Intelligence \
Systems

Introduction:
In a futuristic world where technology has reached unprecedented levels\
, artificial intelligence has become an integral part of everyday life.
 However, a critical bug has emerged, resulting in widespread failures
of AI systems globally. This report outlines the initial steps taken to
 solve the bug, including clues discovered and obstacles faced during t
he investigation.

1. Investigation Phase:
The first step in addressing the critical bug was to launch a comprehen\
sive investigation into its root cause. The development team, in collab
oration with AI experts and system administrators, undertook the follow
ing initial actions:

a. Analyzing System Logs: System logs were reviewed to identify any err\
ors, abnormal behaviors, or anomalies recorded before the bug manifeste
d. Clues included sudden spikes in computational usage, unexpected data
 input/output patterns, and crashes.

b. Testing and Reproduction: Efforts were made to reproduce the bug und\
er controlled testing environments to better understand its triggers an
d effects. Various scenarios were explored, including input manipulatio
n and pattern recognition stress tests.

c. Bug Reporting and User Feedback Analysis: Users and system administr\
ators were encouraged to provide detailed bug reports and feedback. The
se reports were crucial in gaining insights into the specific instances
 where the failures occurred and understanding potential patterns.

2. Clues Discovered:
During the investigation phase, several key clues came to light:

a. Timing Patterns: The bug seemed to exhibit a time-dependent behavior\

, suggesting it was triggered at specific intervals or under certain co
nditions.

b. Data Input Verification: Preliminary analysis indicated that the bug\
 might be associated with the way AI systems processed and verified dat
a inputs.

c. System Interactions: Instances of system failures were found to be m\
ore frequent when AI systems interacted with each other, suggesting the
 possibility of a cross-system interaction bug.

3. Obstacles Faced:
While progress was made during the early stages of the investigation, t\
he team encountered some obstacles:

a. Complexity: The bug's complexity posed a significant challenge, as i\
t affected multiple layers of AI systems and their interdependencies.

b. Limited Debugging Tools: Existing debugging tools were not designed \
to handle such complex bug scenarios, making it difficult to trace the
root cause.

c. Massive Data Sets: The massive amounts of data processed by AI syste\
ms made it challenging to identify specific patterns or trigger points
associated with the bug.

Conclusion:
In summary, the initial steps to solve the critical bug in AI systems i\
nvolved conducting a thorough investigation, analyzing system logs, and
 soliciting bug reports from users and system administrators. Clues dis
covered during this phase, such as timing patterns and data input verif
ication issues, provided valuable insights into the bug's behavior. Nev
ertheless, the team faced obstacles such as complexity, inadequate debu
gging tools, and the sheer volume of data to overcome. These initial st
eps set the foundation for a further in-depth analysis and systematic a
pproach to resolving the bug, ensuring the restoration of AI systems to

```
their full functionality.
```

18.4: Use role-playing

Ask the model to play the role of a specific expert or professional. This helps to tailor the response to your needs.

Example:

```
In a futuristic world where technology has reached unimaginable heights\
, artificial intelligence has been integrated into every aspect of dail
y life. However, a critical bug suddenly occurs, causing massive failur
es in AI systems around the world.

As an AI expert, you are tasked with finding the source of the bug and \
fixing it before the company plunges into chaos.

Write a detailed report describing the first steps of your investigatio\
n, including clues you have discovered and obstacles you have encounter
ed along the way.
```

Output:

```
Investigation Report: AI System Failure

Date: [Insert Date]
Investigator: Felix AI

Summary:
I have been assigned as the AI expert to investigate and resolve the cr\
itical bug causing widespread failures in AI systems across the world.
The situation is critical, as the bug has led to chaos and disruption i
n various sectors that heavily depend on AI integration. This report ou
tlines the initial steps taken in the investigation, along with the clu
```

es discovered and obstacles encountered.

1. Initial Assessment:
Upon receiving the assignment, I immediately gathered information from \
company databases, discussions with affected stakeholders, and analysis
 reports. It became evident that the bug was affecting both hardware an
d software components of AI systems, leading to a partial or complete s
ystem failure.

2. Preliminary Indicators:
a) Widespread System Failures: The bug was observed to be widespread ac\
ross various geographical locations and industries, affecting AI system
s ranging from autonomous vehicles to healthcare diagnostics. This indi
cated a virus-like propagation capability or a centralized point of vul
nerability.
b) Symptom Patterns: The failures displayed common symptoms such as sys\
tem freeze, inability to process data, and undesired behavior. This sug
gested that the bug may be embedded within a common module or framework
 used in the affected AI systems.

3. Database Analysis:
An in-depth analysis of AI system databases, logs, and error reports wa\
s conducted. The key observations include:
a) Unusual Code Sequences: Instances of anomalous code sequences were d\
iscovered in the AI system logs, indicating potential hijacking or inje
ction of malicious code.
b) Experimental Modules: Certain AI systems had experimental modules im\
plemented for research purposes, suggesting that the bug might have ori
ginated from an untested component within the AI architecture.

4. Collaborative Investigation:
Recognizing the magnitude of the issue, a task force was assembled with\
 experts from diverse fields such as cybersecurity, software engineerin
g, and AI framework development. Regular meetings were scheduled to exc
hange findings, share insights, and identify potential leads.

5. Obstacles:
a) Complexity of AI Systems: The complexity of the AI systems presented\
 a significant obstacle, as they encompassed extensive codebases, intri
cate algorithms, and interdependent modules. Analyzing such complex sys
tems required high computational resources and time constraints.
b) Encrypted Communication Channels: Due to the high-level security pro\
tocols implemented in AI systems, investigating encrypted communication
 channels became a challenge. Accessing communication logs and analyzin
g data transmission paths required extensive cooperation from relevant
stakeholders.
c) False Leads: Several false leads were encountered during the initial\
 investigation phase, leading to delays and diversion of resources. Att
ention to detail and a systematic approach were crucial in separating g
enuine clues from noise.

6. Next Steps:
Based on the initial findings, the following steps will be taken to pro\
gress the investigation:
a) Code Review: A comprehensive review of the AI system's codebase will\
 be conducted, scrutinizing each component for vulnerabilities or irreg
ularities.
b) Dependencies Analysis: An in-depth analysis of dependencies, includi\
ng external libraries and frameworks, will be performed to identify pot
ential weak points.
c) Reverse Engineering: Efforts will be made to reverse-engineer the bu\
g in isolated test environments to understand the root cause and assess
 its propagation behavior.
d) Data Forensics: Forensic analysis of infected systems will be conduc\
ted to retrieve metadata and trace the bug's point of entry.

Conclusion:
The initial steps of the investigation have unearthed crucial clues, in\
dicating potential vectors and weak points in the AI system architectur
e. While considerable challenges exist, the collaborative task force an
d systematic approach will help navigate through them. Further analysis
 and investigation will be conducted to identify the source of the bug

and pave the way for a solution to restore AI systems worldwide.

(end of report)

18.5: Use references

If you want the model to imitate a specific writing style or voice, mention it in your prompt. This allows the model to generate responses that match your desired style.

For example, if you want the model to respond like Shakespeare, you can include instructions such as:

Write a review of the movie "Avatar" in the style of Shakespeare.

Output:

Hark! Pray lend me thy ear, for I shall recite

A tale of wondrous sights that do delight.

"Avatar" it be, a film of grand scale,

Whose beauty and depth doth never fail.

In Pandora's land, a conflict doth grow,

Twixt humans and Na'vi, 'tis a tale of woe.

A Marine named Jake, with legs no longer whole,

Embarks on a mission, a story to unfold.

Through the eyes of Nav'i, he doth take flight,

With blue skin and tail, a mystical sight.

The land of Pandora, so vibrant and alive,

With forests and creatures that doth thrive.

Yet greed and ambition cloud human hearts,

For they seek to plunder and tear apart.

With the use of avatars, in flesh they dwell,

To win the trust of Na'vi, 'tis Jake's spell.

He meets fair Neytiri, a warrior strong and true,

Their love blossoms amidst the strife they pursue.

But war it doth beckon, like a thunderous roar,

As humans attack Pandora, seeking to explore.

The battle commences, with swords and machines,

In a clash of cultures, with tragic scenes.

Shakespearean tragedy, it doth unfold,

As friendships are broken and lives are sold.

But hope doth prevail, as Jake takes a stand,

To fight for the Na'vi and protect their land.

With unity and courage, they rise as one,

To defeat the humans and see justice done.

"Avatar's" tale, like a play on the stage,

Doth delve into themes that doth never age.

Man's arrogance and the cost of his greed,

The power of love and unity, indeed.

In Pandora's world, we find a reflection,

Of our own earth's plight, with deep introspection.

So let me end this review with a decree,

"Avatar" is a masterpiece, for all to see.

18.6: Use double quotes

If you want to emphasize certain words or phrases in your prompt, use double quotes. This could help the model understand the importance or specific focus of those words.

Example:

Can you provide a very short explanation of the "benefits" and "limitat\
ions" of renewable energy sources?

ChatGPT output:

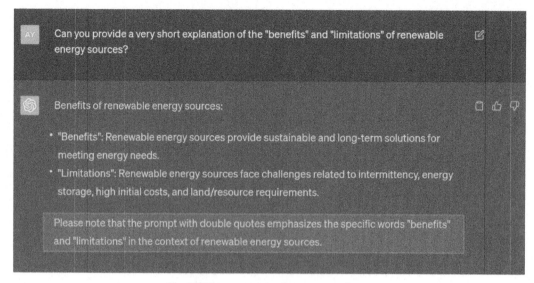

ChatGPT response to the prompt above

API output:

```
Certainly!

Benefits of renewable energy sources:
1. Environmental impact: Renewable energy sources generate electricity \
without producing harmful greenhouse gas emissions, reducing air pollut
ion and mitigating climate change.
2. Energy sustainability: Renewable energy is infinite and abundant, me\
aning it will not deplete over time like fossil fuels. This helps to en
sure a consistent and long-term energy supply.
3. Job creation: The renewable energy industry creates jobs, both direc\
tly in manufacturing and installation and indirectly in support service
s and related sectors.
4. Cost savings: Over time, renewable energy sources can lead to reduce\
d energy costs as technology advances and economies of scale are achiev
ed.

Limitations of renewable energy sources:
1. Intermittency: Some renewable sources, such as solar and wind, are d\
```

ependent on weather conditions. This intermittency can be challenging t
o manage, requiring grid infrastructure upgrades and energy storage sol
utions.
2. Initial costs: The upfront costs of installing renewable energy syst\
ems can be higher compared to traditional fossil fuel-based systems. Ho
wever, costs have been decreasing over time as technology improves.
3. Land and resource requirements: Certain renewable energy sources, li\
ke solar panels and wind turbines, require significant land space and s
pecific geographic conditions. This can sometimes lead to conflicts ove
r land use.
4. Geographic limitations: Not all regions have access to the same rene\
wable energy sources, making it challenging to achieve a complete trans
ition to renewables in some areas.

I hope this brief explanation helps you understand the benefits and lim\
itations of renewable energy sources. Let me know if you have any furth
er questions!

18.7: Use single quotes when needed

Use single quotes to indicate a quote within a quote. This helps the model understand the context of the quote and generate a relevant response.

Example:

Write an essay titled "An analysis of the poem 'The Road Not Taken' by \
Robert Frost".

This prompt instructs the model to write an essay with the title "An analysis of the
poem 'The Road Not Taken' by Robert Frost."

The double quotes are used to indicate the title of the essay, while the single quotes
are used to denote the specific title of the poem within the essay title.

Output:

Title: An Analysis of the Poem "The Road Not Taken" by Robert Frost

Introduction:
"The Road Not Taken" is one of Robert Frost's most widely recognized an\
d anthologized poems. Published in 1916, it explores themes of decision
-making, individuality, and the uncertainty of life's choices. Through
vivid imagery and thoughtful introspection, Frost brilliantly captures
the complexities of human existence and the profound impact of choices
made along life's journey.

Theme of Individuality and Decision-Making:
One of the central themes in "The Road Not Taken" is the concept of ind\
ividuality. The poem follows a speaker who is faced with a crucial deci
sion: which path to take in a forest. Frost masterfully uses the metaph
or of the two diverging roads to symbolize life's various choices and t
he unique paths each individual must navigate. The poem encourages read
ers to reflect upon their own choices and the significance they hold in
 shaping their lives. Frost reminds us that choosing the less-traveled
path, though it may seem daunting, can lead to individuality and person
al growth.

Uncertainty and Regret:
Another significant theme in the poem is the uncertainty and regret tha\
t accompanies decision-making. The speaker laments that "way leads on t
o way" and that once a path is chosen, the option to explore the other
disappears. Frost's words evoke a sense of longing and contemplation, h
inting at the missed opportunities and what might have been. The regret
ful tone in the final stanza, where the speaker acknowledges the diffic
ulty of predicting the consequences of our choices, adds a touch of mel
ancholy to the poem.

Metaphorical Imagery:
Frost's use of vivid and metaphorical imagery throughout the poem enhan\
ces its depth and impact. The fork in the road symbolizes a momentous d
ecision, while the two paths represent life's possibilities. The speake
r observes that one road appeared "grassy and wanted wear," suggesting

it was less traveled and thus more enticing. This highlights the human inclination to seek uniqueness and diverge from the conventional. Frost 's vivid descriptions of the surrounding nature, such as "yellow wood," "undergrowth," and "leaves no step had trodden black," further immerse the reader in the speaker's contemplative journey.

Multiple Interpretations:
"The Road Not Taken" is a poem that invites multiple interpretations. S\ ome readers interpret it as an exploration of the choices one makes in life and the resulting consequences. Others interpret it as a commentar y on societal pressure and conformity. The ambiguity of the poem, combi ned with Frost's skillful use of language, encourages readers to intros pect and contemplate their own choices, experiences, and desires.

Conclusion:
"The Road Not Taken" by Robert Frost remains one of the most beloved an\ d widely studied poems of all time. Its exploration of themes such as i ndividuality, decision-making, uncertainty, and regret strikes a chord with readers from various walks of life. Through metaphorical imagery a nd introspective reflection, Frost reminds us of the importance of embr acing our individuality and recognizing the profound impact our choices can have on our lives. The poem serves as a timeless reminder that lif e ultimately consists of a series of choices and that the roads we take can shape our journey in unforeseen ways.

18.8: Use text separators

Use text separators such as """ and === to separate different sections of your prompt. This helps the model understand the structure of your prompt and generate a relevant response.

Example:

Translate the following title from English to Welsh, Afrikaans, and Ara\
bic:

"""
An analysis of the poem 'The Road Not Taken' by Robert Frost
"""

Output:

Sure!

Here's the translation of the title "An analysis of the poem 'The Road \
Not Taken' by Robert Frost" into Welsh, Afrikaans, and Arabic:

Welsh: Dadansoddiad o'r gerdd 'The Road Not Taken' gan Robert Frost
Afrikaans: 'n Analise van die gedig 'The Road Not Taken' deur Robert Fr\
ost
Arabic: □□□□□ □□□□□ □□□□□□" □□□□ □□ "□□□□ □□□□□□ □□□□□

Let me know if there's anything else I can assist you with!

18.9: Be specific

Give specific details in your prompt to avoid vague or generic responses. The more
specific your instructions are, the better the response will be.

Example:

Write a compelling cover letter to apply for a marketing manager positi\
on at a technology company based in San Francisco. Mention your relevan
t experience in digital marketing, your team management skills, and you
r passion for technological innovation. Also include your short and lon
g term career goals, as well as the reasons why you want to work specif
ically for this company.

By giving specific details such as the position, location, required skills, and motivations, you give the model clear information about what you expect from the response. This allows it to generate a personalized cover letter tailored to your needs, highlighting relevant aspects of your professional profile and demonstrating your specific interest in this company.

Output:

```
[Your Name]
[Your Address]
[City, State, ZIP Code]
[Email Address]
[Phone Number]
[Date]

[Company Name]
[Company Address]
[City, State, ZIP Code]

Dear Hiring Manager,

I am writing to express my strong interest in the Marketing Manager pos\
ition at your esteemed technology company based in San Francisco. As an
 accomplished digital marketing professional with a passion for technol
ogical innovation, I believe my skills and experience make me an ideal
candidate for this role.

With [X] years of experience in digital marketing, I have developed a c\
omprehensive understanding of various marketing channels and strategies
. My expertise includes social media marketing, content marketing, SEO,
 SEM, and email marketing. I have successfully planned and implemented
digital marketing campaigns that resulted in increased brand visibility
, higher customer engagement, and improved lead generation for the comp
anies I have worked with.

One of my proudest achievements was managing a team of talented marketi\
ng professionals at my previous position. I believe in fostering an env
```

ironment of collaboration and empowerment, which allowed my team to con
sistently deliver exceptional results. I am adept at identifying each t
eam member's strengths and leveraging them to maximize productivity and
 overall performance.

In addition to my expertise in digital marketing and team management, I\
 am genuinely passionate about technological innovation. I constantly s
trive to stay updated with the latest trends and advancements in the te
ch industry, ensuring that my marketing strategies align with the ever-
changing landscape. This passion drives me to think creatively, adapt q
uickly, and experiment with new strategies to achieve business objectiv
es.

My short-term goal is to lead a dynamic marketing team, leveraging my s\
kills and experience to contribute to the growth of a forward-thinking
technology company. In the long term, I aspire to take on broader leade
rship roles within the organization, driving strategic initiatives that
 have a profound impact on the company's success.

Your company, with its reputation for innovation and commitment to push\
ing boundaries in the technology industry, aligns perfectly with my car
eer goals and passion. I greatly admire your achievements in creating c
utting-edge products and services that have revolutionized the market.
With my expertise in digital marketing and my drive for technological p
rogress, I am confident that I can contribute significantly to your com
pany's success.

Thank you for considering my application. I would welcome the opportuni\
ty to discuss how my skills and experience align with your company's ne
eds in further detail. I have attached my resume for your review.

I look forward to the possibility of joining your visionary team and ma\
king meaningful contributions to your continued growth and success.

Yours sincerely,

[Your Name]

18.10: Give examples

If you already have documents, articles, text excerpts, or examples that you want the model to follow or that serve as inspiration, feel free to include them in your prompt. This allows the model to generate responses in a style or manner similar to these references. You can use relevant excerpts from articles, quotes from renowned authors, or specific passages that illustrate the desired tone or content.

Example:

```
Here is the review from the Times:


"""
The good surprise is that Avatar deserves all the effort its sponsors p\
ut into it. James Cameron is definitely a great storyteller, and Avatar
 is a fabulous film in every sense of the word. It takes us into the ne
ar future, to a stunningly beautiful planet called Pandora, where the g
round is rich in a mineral that would mean the end of the energy crisis
 on Earth... Its inhabitants, the Na'vi, are tall athletic creatures wi
th blue skin, and they strive to fend off the assaults of industrial gr
oups that send hordes of settlers to the planet.
The story adopts the perspective of one of them: a marine with paralyze\
d legs who is offered the opportunity to "walk" again in this lush para
dise. We won't explain why or how, so as not to spoil the joy of discov
ery. However, we can reveal that this soldier has a heart bigger than h
is backpack, and he may well become an ally to those he is ordered to a
ttack...
Cameron, a popular filmmaker, tells timeless stories that, as soon as w\
e become aware of them, resonate with current debates. Avatar could thu
s provide some answers to those who question us about nationality or cr
iteria for belonging to a group or country. It can also be seen as a pa
cifist allegory at a time when the United States is mired in Afghanista
n, with the film taking the side of the victims of all wars ("but not t
```

```
he Taliban," the filmmaker said in a press conference on Monday). Like
Little Big Man in the past or Terrence Malick's The New World more rece
ntly, Avatar defends human values without preaching or risking ridicule
. It goes even further by bringing animism back into the spotlight: yes
, the entire nature is believed to have a soul, and that indeed makes u
s dream again.
"""
```

```
Now, write a similar film very short review for: Inception
```

Output:

```
Here is a short review for "Inception":
```

```
Inception is a mind-bending cinematic masterpiece that takes us on a jo\
urney through the realms of dreams. Directed by Christopher Nolan, this
  film combines superb storytelling with stunning visuals. It explores t
he concept of dream infiltration and manipulation, where skilled indivi
duals navigate through layers of consciousness. With a talented cast an
d an intricate plot, Inception keeps viewers on the edge of their seats
, questioning reality until the very end. It is a thought-provoking and
  thrilling experience that will leave you captivated.
```

18.11: Indicate the desired response length

Specify the desired response length in your prompt. This allows the model to understand whether you want a short and concise response or a more detailed explanation.

Example:

```
Develop the topic 'Well-being and meditation' in 200 words.
```

Output:

Well-being and meditation go hand in hand as they are closely linked to\
 each other. Well-being refers to the state of being comfortable, conte
nt, and happy in all aspects of one's life. It encompasses physical, me
ntal, and emotional health, as well as a sense of purpose and fulfillme
nt. On the other hand, meditation is a practice that involves focusing
one's attention and eliminating the stream of thoughts to achieve a men
tally clear and emotionally calm state.

Meditation has been practiced for thousands of years and has been prove\
n to have numerous benefits on one's well-being. Firstly, it helps redu
ce stress and anxiety. Through meditation, individuals can learn to qui
et their minds and let go of the worries and negative thoughts that oft
en contribute to stress and anxiety. This leads to a greater sense of c
alm and relaxation.

Furthermore, meditation improves mental clarity and decision-making. By\
 practicing mindfulness, individuals can develop a heightened sense of
awareness and focus, allowing them to make better choices and be more p
resent in their daily lives. This, in turn, enhances cognitive function
 and boosts productivity.

In terms of physical health, meditation has been found to have positive\
 effects on the immune system, cardiovascular health, and pain manageme
nt. Regular meditation practice has been shown to reduce blood pressure
, lower heart rate, and strengthen the body's ability to fight off illn
esses.

Meditation also plays a crucial role in enhancing emotional well-being.\
 It helps individuals cultivate self-awareness, acceptance, and compass
ion. By observing their thoughts and emotions without judgment, individ
uals can develop a greater understanding of themselves and their emotio
ns, leading to improved self-esteem and overall emotional resilience.

In conclusion, the practice of meditation is an essential tool for prom\
oting overall well-being. It has profound effects on both physical and
mental health, reducing stress, improving focus and decision-making, an

```
d enhancing emotional well-being. Incorporating regular meditation into
 one's daily routine can lead to a happier, healthier, and more fulfill
ing life.
```

The output contains 320 words, which is more than the requested 200 words but it is still a resonable length. LLMs including GPT models are not that good at following instructions that limits the number of words or characters in the response but they try to do their best.

Limiting by number of sentences could work better:

Example:

```
Develop the topic 'Well-being and meditation' in 4 sentences.
```

```
Well-being and meditation are closely interconnected as practicing medi\
tation is known to promote overall well-being. Meditation has been foun
d to reduce stress and anxiety, improve focus and concentration, and en
hance feelings of happiness and contentment. Regular meditation practic
e has also been associated with improved physical health, including low
er blood pressure and improved immune function. By incorporating medita
tion into our daily routine, we can actively cultivate a sense of well-
being and experience its positive impacts on our mental, emotional, and
 physical health.
```

The output contains 4 sentences as requested.

18.12: Guide the model

In some situations, it is important to provide clear instructions and constraints to guide the model. This includes telling the AI what to do, what to avoid, or what to prioritize.

For example, if you want the model to generate a paragraph on a specific topic, you can specify the key points to cover and the information to include.

Example:

Write a 100-word paragraph on the benefits of yoga for mental health. F\
ocus on the calming effect of yoga on the nervous system, stress reduct
ion, and improved concentration and mental clarity. Avoid talking about
 the physical aspects of yoga, and focus only on the aspects related to
 mental health.

Output:

Yoga offers numerous benefits for mental health, primarily through its \
calming effect on the nervous system. By engaging in controlled breathi
ng and gentle movements, yoga helps activate the body's relaxation resp
onse, which can reduce stress and anxiety levels. This practice also pr
omotes mindfulness, enabling individuals to become more present in the
moment and cultivate a greater sense of inner peace. Through regular pr
actice, individuals may experience improved concentration and mental cl
arity, as yoga encourages focus and trains the mind to let go of distra
ctions. Ultimately, yoga serves as a powerful tool in managing mental h
ealth by providing a safe and holistic approach to relaxation and self-
care.

By giving clear instructions and specifying what you want to see included or
excluded, you guide the model in the desired direction and get more targeted
and relevant responses. This allows you to get results that better match your
expectations and the specific needs of your project or interaction with the AI.

Example:

Create a 500 calorie Mediterranean meal plan for one week, for dinner o\
nly. Do not offer me any vegetarian options. Offer me a cheatmeal on Sa
turday night. It should be a diet rich in lean protein with carbohydrat
es (30%), protein (40%), fiber (20%) and fat (10%).

Output:

Sure! Here's a 500-calorie Mediterranean meal plan for one week, focusi\
ng on lean protein, carbohydrates, fiber, and healthy fats. Please note
 that portion sizes may vary, so adjust accordingly to meet your calori
e and macronutrient goals:

Monday:
- Grilled chicken breast (4 oz) with lemon and herbs
- Quinoa (1/2 cup) with roasted vegetables (broccoli, zucchini, and bel\
l peppers)
- Mixed greens salad with cherry tomatoes, cucumbers, and olives, dress\
ed with olive oil and vinegar

Tuesday:
- Baked salmon fillet (4 oz) with a squeeze of lemon
- Brown rice (1/2 cup) with steamed spinach and garlic
- Grilled asparagus spears

Wednesday:
- Lemon garlic shrimp skewers (4 oz) served with roasted cauliflower
- Whole wheat couscous (1/2 cup) with roasted red bell peppers and feta\
 cheese
- Greek salad with lettuce, tomatoes, cucumbers, red onions, and a spri\
nkle of feta cheese, dressed with olive oil and lemon juice

Thursday:
- Grilled lean steak (4 oz) with chimichurri sauce
- Sweet potato wedges (1 small sweet potato) with a sprinkle of paprika
- Grilled zucchini strips

Friday:
- Baked white fish fillet (4 oz) with a squeeze of lime
- Quinoa (1/2 cup) with sautéed mushrooms, onions, and garlic
- Steamed broccoli florets

Saturday:
- **Cheatmeal** (Enjoy your favorite indulgent meal within your calorie\

```
limit)
```

Sunday:
- Grilled chicken kebabs (4 oz) with cherry tomatoes and bell peppers
- Whole wheat pasta (1/2 cup) cooked with garlic, cherry tomatoes, and \
spinach
- Greek salad with lettuce, cucumbers, red onions, and a sprinkle of fe\
ta cheese, dressed with olive oil and lemon juice

Remember to drink plenty of water throughout the day and listen to your\
  body's hunger/fullness cues. Maintaining a balanced and varied diet is
  essential for overall health. Enjoy your meals!

18.13: Don't hesitate to refine

If you need to clarify or refine your prompt further after receiving an initial response, feel free to do so. It is helpful to iterate and refine your instructions to get the desired result.

Example:

After using the following prompt:

```
Create a 500 calorie Mediterranean meal plan for one week, for dinner o\
nly. Do not offer me any vegetarian options. Offer me a cheatmeal on Sa
turday night. It should be a diet rich in lean protein with carbohydrat
es (30%), protein (40%), fiber (20%) and fat (10%).
```

You can refine your prompt further to get a more specific response:

```
Dessert is optional.
```

gpt-3.5-turbo will then generate a new response that takes this new information into account.

18.14: Consider looking at your problem from a different angle

In some cases, it may be helpful to look at your problem from a different angle. This can help you find a new approach to your problem and get a more relevant response.

Example:

```
Summarize the following article in 100 words. Don't include sentences l\
ike "This article is about" or "This article talks about". Instead, foc
us on the key points of the article and the main arguments.


"""
[text of the article]
"""
```

This prompt works fine, except that in some cases, the model may generate a response that includes the sentences "This article is about" or "This article talks about". This is because the model is trying to summarize the article and these sentences are often found at the beginning of a summary. To avoid this, you can try to look at your problem from a different angle and ask the model to rewrite the article instead of summarizing it.

```
You are a journalist and you have to rewrite the following article in y\
our own words without changing the meaning. The article should be 100 w
ords long.


"""
[text of the article]
"""
```

18.15: Consider opening another chat (ChatGPT)

This is very specific to the usage of ChatGPT. With ChatGPT, you have the option to create a new chat, every chat represents a new discussion context.

If you are not satisfied with the response you receive from the model, you can try opening another discussion thread. This will allow you to get a new response from the model, which may be more relevant.

ChatGPT may get stuck in a loop when generating a response that is not relevant to the prompt. This occurs because it tries to find a response related to the previous one, but this is not possible if the previous response is not relevant to the prompt. In such situations, it is best to start a new chat and obtain a fresh response from the model.

18.16: Use the right words and phrases

It is important to use the right words in your prompt. LLMs are trained on vast amounts of text data, which means they have a wide vocabulary at their disposal. By using precise and specific language in your prompt, you can guide the model towards generating more accurate and relevant responses.

For example, instead of asking a general question like "What is the meaning of life?", you can provide more context and specificity in your prompt by asking something like "Can you provide philosophical perspectives on the purpose of human existence?" This helps set the tone and direction for the response and increases the likelihood of receiving a thoughtful and insightful answer.

18.17: Experiment and iterate

Dr. Andrew Ng, a globally recognized leader in AI, said once:

> When I train a machine learning model, it almost never works in the firt time. In fact, I'm very surprised that the first model I trained works. I

think when prompting, the odds of it working the first time is maybe a little bit higher, but it doesn't matter if the first prompt works, what matters most is the process for getting the prompts that works for your application.

The art of prompt engineering involves experimentation and iteration. It's a process of refining and adjusting your prompts based on the generated responses. By observing the model's behavior and iteratively refining your prompts, you can gradually improve the quality and relevance of the generated output.

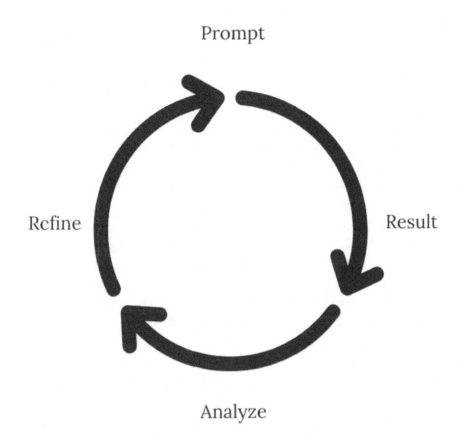

Iterative process of prompt engineering

Remember to evaluate the generated responses critically, consider multiple perspectives, and continue to experiment with different phrasings and approaches to elicit the desired information or insights from the model.

Let's take an example

Write a 100-word paragraph on the benefits of yoga for mental health. F\
ocus on the calming effect of yoga on the nervous system, stress reduct
ion, and improved concentration and mental clarity. Avoid talking about
 the physical aspects of yoga, and focus only on the aspects related to
 mental health.

Output:

Yoga has numerous benefits for mental health, primarily through its cal\
ming effect on the nervous system. Through slow and controlled movement
s, combined with deep breathing exercises, yoga helps activate the body
's relaxation response, reducing stress and anxiety. This, in turn, imp
roves sleep, enhances mood, and boosts overall mental well-being. Moreo
ver, regular practice of yoga helps to improve concentration and mental
 clarity. By cultivating mindfulness and a present-moment awareness, in
dividuals can better focus their attention, leading to increased produc
tivity and improved cognitive functions. Ultimately, yoga provides a ho
listic approach to mental health, offering respite from the demands of
modern life and promoting a balanced state of mind.

This response is quite good but it could be improved by adding more details and
examples. Let's try to refine our prompt to get a more detailed response.

Write a 200-word paragraph on the benefits of yoga for mental health. F\
ocus on the calming effect of yoga on the nervous system, stress reduct
ion, and improved concentration and mental clarity. Avoid talking about
 the physical aspects of yoga, and focus only on the aspects related to
 mental health. Give examples of specific yoga poses that can help redu
ce stress and anxiety, such as child's pose, downward-facing dog, and c
orpse pose.

Output:

Yoga offers significant benefits for mental health, primarily through i\
ts calming effect on the nervous system. By focusing on deep breathing
and slow, deliberate movements, yoga helps to activate the parasympathe
tic nervous system, which is responsible for inducing relaxation and re
ducing stress. This calming effect has been proven to alleviate symptom
s of anxiety and depression, promoting a sense of peace and well-being.

One of the key advantages of yoga for mental health is its ability to r\
educe stress. Through the practice of specific poses such as child's po
se, downward-facing dog, and corpse pose, individuals can release tensi
on and stretch the muscles, leading to a decrease in stress levels. The
se poses promote deep relaxation, allowing individuals to let go of wor
ries and tensions that may be affecting their mental well-being.

In addition to stress reduction, yoga also improves concentration and m\
ental clarity. The focused breathing and precise movements involved in
yoga demand concentration, which can enhance cognitive function and hel
p to clear the mind of distractions. As a result, individuals often fin
d that they are better able to concentrate on tasks and experience impr
oved mental clarity both during and after a yoga session.

In conclusion, yoga provides numerous mental health benefits by calming\
 the nervous system, reducing stress, and enhancing concentration and m
ental clarity. By incorporating yoga poses such as child's pose, downwa
rd-facing dog, and corpse pose into a regular practice, individuals can
 experience a profound positive impact on their mental well-being.

This response is much more detailed and includes specific examples of yoga poses
that can help reduce stress and anxiety. If we want the model to change the tone
of the response to be more positive and uplifting, we can refine our prompt further
by adding instructions such as "Use positive and uplifting language" or "Use words
like 'joyful', 'peaceful', and 'relaxed' ".

Write a 200-word paragraph on the benefits of yoga for mental health. F\
ocus on the calming effect of yoga on the nervous system, stress reduct
ion, and improved concentration and mental clarity. Avoid talking about

the physical aspects of yoga, and focus only on the aspects related to
mental health. Give examples of specific yoga poses that can help redu
ce stress and anxiety, such as child's pose, downward-facing dog, and c
orpse pose. Use positive and uplifting language. Use words like 'joyful
', 'peaceful', and 'relaxed'.

Output:

Yoga has numerous benefits for mental health, providing a soothing and \
calming effect on the nervous system. By engaging in gentle movements,
deep breathing, and meditation, yoga helps to alleviate stress and prom
ote a sense of inner peace. It offers a sanctuary from the hustle and b
ustle of daily life, allowing individuals to reconnect with themselves
and find solace in the present moment. Through regular practice, yoga c
ultivates a more relaxed and tranquil state of mind.

One of the remarkable benefits of yoga is its ability to reduce stress \
levels. By consciously directing attention to the breath and focusing o
n the body in various poses, practitioners experience a release of tens
ion and an easing of anxiety. For instance, the child's pose, where one
 rests their forehead on the ground and gently stretches their arms for
ward, provides a comforting position that encourages deep relaxation. S
imilarly, the downward-facing dog pose allows for an inversion of the b
ody, promoting blood flow to the brain and enhancing mental clarity. Th
e final pose, Corpse pose, is particularly powerful for calming the min
d, inducing a state of deep relaxation and inner stillness.

Beyond stress reduction, yoga improves concentration and mental clarity\
. By quieting the mind and calming the nervous system, individuals expe
rience enhanced focus and clarity of thought. This increased mental acu
ity not only supports productivity and creativity but also helps indivi
duals make better decisions, solve problems more effectively, and navig
ate challenges with a sense of grace and ease.

Overall, the practice of yoga facilitates a joyful and peaceful state o\
f being, allowing individuals to alleviate stress, find mental clarity,

and promote overall well-being. It is a powerful tool for cultivating a relaxed and harmonious mind in today's fast-paced and demanding world .

18.18: Stay mindful of LLMs limitations

While LLMs like GPT-3.5 and GPT-4 have shown impressive capabilities, it's important to recognize their limitations. They are language models trained on existing data and may not always provide accurate or factual information. They can generate plausible-sounding responses but may lack real-world understanding or context.

A good example of a limitation shown by LLMs is their inability in some cases to solve some symbolic and arithmetic problems.

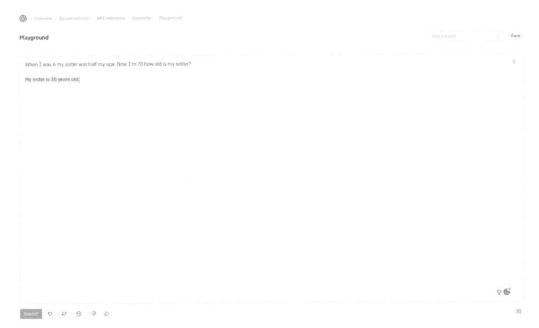

ChatGPT response to an arithmetic problem

Using OpenAI playground[73], we can see that text-davinci-003 is unable to guess the right age using this prompt:

---

[73]https://platform.openai.com/playground?mode=complete

```
Human: When I was 6 my sister was half my age. Now I'm 70 how old is my\
  sister?
AI: My sister is 35 years old.
```

Knowing that text-davinci-003 is one of the most powerful LLMs available, we can assume that other less powerful models may not be able to solve this problem either.

You can read about more cases, sometimes funny, of some wrong or weird responses generated by LLMs in this GitHub repository[74], this Spreadsheet[75] or this wiki[76].

Therefore, it's important to double-check, cross-verify and fact-check the information obtained from LLMs before considering it as an authoritative source. Critical thinking and human judgment remain essential in assessing the validity and reliability of the generated content.

---

[74]https://github.com/giuven95/chatgpt-failures
[75]https://docs.google.com/spreadsheets/d/1kDSERnROv5FgHbVN8z_bXH9gak2IXRtoqz0nwhrviCw/edit#gid=1302320625
[76]https://github.com/ErnestDavis/LLM-Failures/wiki

19: Where and How Prompt Engineering is Used

Prompt engineering is used in many applications, including:

- Creative writing
- Content generation
- Customer service
- Data analysis
- Academic research
- Language translation
- Natural language interfaces
- Educational applications
- Marketing and advertising
- Virtual assistants and smart devices
- Game development
- Healthcare and medical research
- Story generation and role-playing
- Business intelligence and analytics
- Language tutoring and learning
- Image generation
- And more

In this section, we'll take a look at the most common applications of prompt engineering.

19.1: Creative writing

Authors, writers, and content creators use prompt engineering to generate creative ideas, brainstorm storylines, and develop engaging narratives with the assistance of AI language models.

Examples of creative writing applications include:

- AI Storyteller[77]: A tool that uses GPT-3 to generate story ideas and story outlines.
- NovelAI[78]: A service for AI-assisted authorship, storytelling and virtual companionship.

19.2: Content generation, SEO, marketing and advertising

Prompt engineering is largely used in content marketing, social media management, website content creation. Marketers and bloggers use prompt engineering to craft persuasive posts, advertising copies and marketing campaigns.

Below are some examples of applications where prompt engineering can be used to generate SEO, marketing and advertising contents:

- Jasper[79]: Jasper is a comprehensive solution for generating marketing content using AI. It offers over 50 templates for different types of content, ranging from AI-generated social media profiles to e-commerce product descriptions. This tool allows you to create content in three simple steps: choose a template, enter the required information, and adjust the output settings. This information may include the title, tone, and description of the content.

---

[77]https://www.aistoryteller.com/
[78]https://novelai.net/
[79]https://www.jasper.ai/

- GrowthBar[80]: GrowthBar is an AI-based writing suite focused on long-form content. You can perform keyword research and generate an SEO-optimized blog plan with just one click. With another click, you can write a complete blog article that adheres to SEO best practices in the GrowthBar editor. GrowthBar works in over 20 languages and also includes keyword research, competitor research, an AI-based chatbot, and a range of other AI-based tools, including a press release generator, an email newsletter generator, and more.
- Rytr[81]: Rytr is an affordable AI content generator with numerous features. Its paid offerings start from $9 per month, but it also offers an unlimited free version with many functionalities.
- Frase[82]: Frase is an AI content generation tool focused on SEO. Its built-in optimization feature provides keyword suggestions based on competitors' content to help your article rank higher in search results.
- Copy.ai[83]: Copy.ai is an all-in-one AI writing tool with over 90 content templates and supports 25 languages. Despite its popularity as a copywriting option, it can also write long-form content such as blog articles.
- Copysmith[84]: Copysmith is an excellent AI tool for generating short content such as ad copies, product descriptions, and slogans. This tool can create up to 15 variations of content with different voices. In addition to generating content based on use cases, Copysmith allows you to automatically rewrite, enhance, or extend your sentences. This is a great feature for auditing existing content.
- Scalenut[85]: Scalenut is an excellent AI writing assistant tool for creating long-form blog articles. You can use it throughout the content production process, from keyword planning to topic research and writing.
- LongShot[86]: AI writers sometimes generate dubious facts that require manual verification. If you need an AI writer that automatically creates content and fact-checks, consider using LongShot.
- Content at Scale[87]: Content at Scale is an AI-driven platform that allows SEO specialists to quickly and efficiently create engaging and high-quality content.

---

[80]https://www.growthbarseo.com/
[81]https://app.rytr.me/
[82]https://www.frase.io/
[83]https://www.copy.ai/
[84]https://copysmith.ai/
[85]https://www.scalenut.com/
[86]https://www.longshot.ai/
[87]https://contentatscale.ai/

Thanks to advanced AI technology, the platform can generate long-form blog articles of over 2,500 words in just five minutes, based on in-depth research. It achieves this by analyzing top-ranking content on Google and combining it to create fully optimized articles. Unlike other AI writing tools, Content at Scale creates content of equivalent quality to that of a human and is entirely original.

These tools work like ChatGPT, they require a prompt and generate content based on it. However, each tool has its own unique features and capabilities, therefore prompting may vary from one tool to another.

19.3: Customer Service

AI-powered chatbots and virtual assistants benefit from prompt engineering to provide relevant and context-aware responses to customer inquiries and support requests. The quality and effectiveness of a chatbot or virtual assistant depends on the quality of the prompts used to train it and its capacity to understand the prompt of the user and generate a relevant response. Chatbots use NLP techniques to analyze the user query.

Before generating a response, the chatbot executes some steps on the query text (normalization). The process of text normalization typically involves several sub-steps:

- **Lowercasing**: Converting all characters to lowercase to ensure consistent comparisons and avoid duplications due to case variations (e.g., "Apple" and "apple" are treated as the same word).
- **Tokenization**: Splitting the text into individual words or tokens to break down the text into smaller units for analysis.
- **Removing punctuation**: Removing punctuation marks (e.g., periods, commas, exclamation marks) to eliminate noise and simplify the text.
- **Expanding contractions**: Expanding contracted forms, such as "can't" to "cannot," "won't" to "will not," etc., to represent the full words and standardize the language.

- **Removing special characters**: Removing special characters, symbols, and emojis from the text to focus on the main content (e.g: HTML tags, emoticons, etc.).
- **Handling numbers**: Converting numerical expressions to words (e.g., "10" to "ten") or removing them entirely, depending on the context and task.
- **Stopword removal**: Eliminating common and non-contextual words, such as "the," "is," "and," etc., that do not add significant meaning to the text.
- **Lemmatization or stemming**: Reducing words to their base or root form (lemmas) to group together variations of the same word (e.g., "running," "runs," "ran" to "run").
- **Handling abbreviations**: Expanding abbreviations to their full forms (e.g., "USA" to "United States of America").
- **Spelling correction**: Correcting spelling mistakes to ensure accurate language processing.

Following is a very basic text normalization function in Python. It uses libraries like nltk and re to perform tasks such as lowercase conversion, tokenization, punctuation removal, and more.

```python
import nltk
import re
from nltk.corpus import stopwords
from nltk.tokenize import word_tokenize

nltk.download('punkt')
nltk.download('stopwords')

def text_normalization(text):
    # Convert text to lowercase
    text = text.lower()

    # Remove punctuation using regular expressions
    text = re.sub(r'[^\w\s]', '', text)

    # Tokenize the text into words
    words = word_tokenize(text)
```

```
# Remove stopwords
stop_words = set(stopwords.words('english'))
words = [word for word in words if word not in stop_words]

# Lemmatization using NLTK's WordNetLemmatizer
lemmatizer = nltk.WordNetLemmatizer()
words = [lemmatizer.lemmatize(word) for word in words]

# Join the words back into a normalized sentence
normalized_text = ' '.join(words)

return normalized_text

# Test the function
input_text = "This is a sample sentence, showing off the stop words fil\
tration."
normalized_text = text_normalization(input_text)
print(normalized_text)
```

Output:

```
sample sentence showing stop word filtration
```

The next steps in the pipeline is intent classification. Intent classification is the process of identifying the intent of the user query. For example, if the user asks "How do I reset my password?", the intent of the query is "password reset."

In an over-simplified way, this code snippet shows how to classify the intent of a user query using a sickit-learn:

```python
from sklearn.feature_extraction.text import TfidfVectorizer
from sklearn.svm import SVC
from sklearn.pipeline import make_pipeline

# Sample data for training
password_queries = [
    "How to reset my password?",
    "I forgot my password.",
    "What is my password?",
    "My password is not working.",
]

non_password_queries = [
    "How to create a new account?",
    "New user registration.",
    "How to delete my account?",
    "Close my account.",
    "I want to open a new account.",
]

# Create labels for the data
password_labels = ["password inquiry"] * len(password_queries)
non_password_labels = ["non-password inquiry"] * len(non_password_queri\
es)

# Combine the data and labels
data = password_queries + non_password_queries
labels = password_labels + non_password_labels

# Create the classifier pipeline
classifier = make_pipeline(TfidfVectorizer(), SVC(kernel='linear'))

# Train the classifier
classifier.fit(data, labels)

# Test the classifier with new queries
```

```
new_queries = [
    "I lost my password, please help.",
    "Can I change my password?",
    "I want to open two accounts. Is it possible?",
    "I want to recover my account.",
]

# Predict the intent for new queries
for query in new_queries:
    prediction = classifier.predict([query])
    print(f"Query: '{query}' => Prediction: {prediction[0]}")
```

Output:

```
Query: 'I lost my password, please help.' => Prediction: password inqui\
ry
Query: 'Can I change my password?' => Prediction: password inquiry
Query: 'I want to open two accounts. Is it possible?' => Prediction: no\
n-password inquiry
Query: 'I want to recover my account.' => Prediction: non-password inqu\
iry
```

As you can see from the basic example above, the classifier is able to correctly identify whether a query is related to password inquiries or not.

The example code uses labeled data for training the classifier. The data should be carefully prepared with clear labels for different intents, i.e., "password inquiry" and "non-password inquiry." in our case. High-quality training data with accurate and diverse examples is crucial for a chatbot to handle a wide range of user queries effectively.

We are also using TF-IDF vectorizer (TfidfVectorizer) from scikit-learn to convert text data into numerical features. This transformation helps in representing the user queries in a format suitable for machine learning algorithms. Then we are using a linear support vector classifier (SVC) to train the model. The choice of classifier depends on the nature of the problem and the data. In this case, SVM is chosen for text classification, and it has been widely used and proven effective for such tasks.

The classifier pipeline is created using `make_pipeline` from scikit-learn. Then we train the classifier using the `fit` method. Finally, we test the classifier with new queries using the `predict` method.

In a real-world scenario, performing error analysis to understand the mistakes made by the classifier and quantifying predictions quality[88] is as important as training the model. This helps in improving the quality of the training data and the classifier itself. As new queries and user interactions occur, the chatbot should be able to continuously learn and adapt to the changes. This could be done using active learning, where the chatbot asks the user for feedback on the quality of the response. The feedback is then used to improve the classifier and the chatbot's response.

19.4: Data analysis, reporting, and visualization

Prompt engineering helps in data exploration and analysis by allowing users to pose complex questions and receive insightful explanations from AI language models.

Let's say you have a dataset of customer reviews for a product, and you want to explore the sentiments expressed by the customers.

- Without prompts: You could use traditional keyword searches like "positive," "negative," or "neutral" to categorize the sentiments, but this may not capture the full complexity of the reviews.
- With prompts: You can use prompts to ask a more specific and nuanced question to the language model, like: "What are the main positive aspects mentioned by customers in the reviews?" or "What common complaints do customers have about the product?"

---

[88] https://scikit-learn.org/stable/modules/model_evaluation.html

By using prompts, the AI model can analyze the dataset and provide more detailed insights, allowing users to gain a deeper understanding of the sentiments expressed by customers and identify specific areas for improvement or further investigation. Prompt engineering best practices can help in designing effective prompts that yield the most relevant and useful results.

19.5: Virtual assistants and smart devices

If you have an Alexa or Google Home device, you've probably used it to ask questions like "What's the weather like today?" or "What's the capital of France?". These devices use basic prompt engineering techniques to understand your questions and provide the most relevant answers. The same applies to other virtual assistants as well, like Siri and Cortana.

With the rise of LLMs, virtual assistants will become more sophisticated and capable of answering more complex questions. For example, Amazon is developing AlexaTM (Alexa Teacher Model) to adapt its virtual assistant capabilities to the age of ChatGPT. Prompt engineering techniques will play a crucial role in making this possible.

19.6: Game development

Game designers and developers use prompt engineering to create dynamic and interactive storytelling experiences in video games.

Charisma[89] is a good example of a platform that uses AI and Natural Language Processing to interpret player responses in order to send players down the most appropriate story path.

If we take an example of an RPG (Role-Playing Game), the player's choices and actions can be used to generate prompts that influence the story and the game world. For example, if the player chooses to be a thief, the game can generate prompts that are relevant to that character's background and skills. If the player chooses to be a mage, the game can generate prompts that are relevant to that character's background and skills.

---

[89]https://charisma.ai/

Imagine a fantasy RPG where the player takes on the role of a brave hero exploring a vast world filled with various quests, challenges, and interactions with NPCs (non-player characters).

The game developers can use prompt engineering to create dynamic and engaging quest interactions. When the player approaches an NPC (non-player characters), instead of presenting a static quest text, the NPC responds differently based on the player's previous actions, in-game achievements, or chosen character traits. The game uses a NLP model with a pre-designed set of prompts to generate personalized quest dialogues. This approach creates a more immersive and interactive experience, as the NPCs adapt their responses to the player's actions and decisions.

Developers may also add prompt-driven quests, dynamic story telling, dialogue options and even character creation to their games. This allows players to live unique and unlimited adventures in a virtual world. This is even more true with the rise of metaveses and virtual worlds.

19.7: Healthcare and medical

Prompt engineering plays a crucial role in advancing healthcare applications through the use of AI and natural language processing. In various healthcare scenarios, such as patient triage and medical information extraction, prompt engineering enables AI-powered chatbots and assistants to collect comprehensive patient data, streamline processes, and provide personalized health education.

By creating effective prompts, AI tools can accurately extract vital medical information from complex health records, helping clinicians make informed decisions. Additionally, prompt engineering empowers AI models to offer empathetic mental health support, encouraging users to share their concerns and providing appropriate guidance and resources.

Through prompt engineering, the efficiency and effectiveness of AI-driven healthcare solutions are enhanced, leading to improved patient outcomes and providing healthcare professionals with valuable insights.

19.8: Story generation and role-playing

Using prompt engineering effectively enhances interactive storytelling experiences and role-playing scenarios in various entertainment applications.

A good example of a tool that uses prompt engineering is AI Dungeon[90], a text-based adventure game that uses AI to generate the story based on the user's input.

19.9: Business intelligence and analytics

Enterprises can use prompt engineering to extract valuable insights from large datasets and make informed decisions. Prompt engineering involves the design and use of carefully crafted prompts to interact with AI language models and retrieve specific information from the data. This approach is particularly valuable when dealing with complex, unstructured data such as text documents, customer feedback, social media posts, or research papers.

Enterprises can leverage prompt engineering to gain insights into various aspects of their businesses. For instance, prompt engineering can be used to analyze customer feedback and sentiments, categorize large volumes of text data, extract information from research surveys, identify emerging trends, generate document summaries, and conduct competitive analysis. By crafting prompts that target specific data points, businesses can make well-informed decisions and adapt their strategies accordingly.

Prompt engineering is a powerful tool that enterprises can use to enhance their data analysis and decision-making capabilities and these are just a few examples. More examples exist depending on the industry such as finance, marketing, and sales.

---

[90]https://play.aidungeon.io/

19.10: Image generation

Several text-to-image models have emerged in recent years, such as DALL-E[91], Stable Diffusion[92], and Midjourney[93]. These models can create images from text prompts, some of them require additional specific instructions to produce desired outputs.

---

[91]https://openai.com/dall-e-2
[92]https://stablediffusionweb.com/
[93]https://www.midjourney.com/

A clownfish swimming in the ocean.   A HDR photo of a crazy clownfish
                                          swimming in the ocean by Alex
                                          Mustard. Sharp, colorful, and
                                          intriguing.

Examples of text-to-image prompts

Prompt engineering is used to guide these models and generate images that are
relevant to the given prompts.

20: Anatomy of a Prompt

When creating a prompt, it is important to understand the different components that you may use in it. The following list describes the different components of a prompt:

- Role
- Instructions
- Input data
- Context
- Rules
- Output
- Examples

There is no official standard for creating prompts, but most prompts contain at least one of these components.

Following is an illustration:

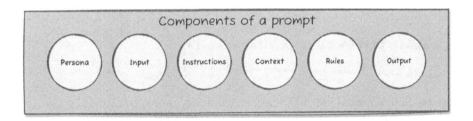

Components of a prompt

Not all of these components are required, but they can be useful in getting more accurate and relevant results.

20.1: Role or persona

A role is a fictional character that represents a specific type of user. It is used to provide context for the prompt and guide the model's response.

Examples of roles include:

- A customer service representative
- A salesperson
- A doctor
- A lawyer
- A teacher

These are some examples:

```
Act as a customer service representative for a large retail company.
```

```
Act as an experienced salesperson.
```

```
You are a clever and friendly assistant. Your job is to help people fin\
d the best deals on the internet.
```

```
Act as a movie critic for a popular website.
```

```
You are an SEO specialist with more than 20 years of experience.
```

A user on Hugging Face has an app based on BART model and trained on a dataset of prompts. The app is called ChatGPT Prompt Generator[94] and it could be helpful to experiment and generate the role of your prompt.

---

[94]https://huggingface.co/spaces/merve/ChatGPT-prompt-generator

20.2: Instructions

The instructions is the main part of the prompt and it provides the main task for the model. Instructions could be used to ask the model to perform a specific task or generate a specific type of output.

This is an example:

```
Create a blog post titled "The Top 10 Movies of All Time".
```

Depending on the prompt type, the instructions could be explicit (e.g. a clear task) or implicit (e.g. a question or a conversation). We are going to learn more about the types of prompts in the next sections.

20.3: Input data

The input data is what we feed to the model and it could be anything from a a few sentences, a list, or a long paragraph. Input data are used to provide the model a guidance on what and how to generate the output.

Let's imagine you want to create a blog post about the top 10 movies of all time according to IMDb. You could assist the AI model by feeding it the following input:

```
1. The Shawshank Redemption
2. The Godfather
3. The Dark Knight
4. The Godfather Part II
5. 12 Angry Men
6. Schindler's List
7. The Lord of the Rings: The Return of the King
8. Pulp Fiction
9. The Lord of the Rings: The Fellowship of the Ring
10. The Good, the Bad and the Ugly
```

If we add the role and the instruction, we get the following prompt:

```
Act as a movie critic for a popular website.

Create a blog post titled "The Top 10 Movies of All Time".

Use the following list of movies as input:

1. The Shawshank Redemption
2. The Godfather
3. The Dark Knight
4. The Godfather Part II
5. 12 Angry Men
6. Schindler's List
7. The Lord of the Rings: The Return of the King
8. Pulp Fiction
9. The Lord of the Rings: The Fellowship of the Ring
10. The Good, the Bad and the Ugly
```

20.4: Context

Adding the context to the prompt is optional, but it can be useful to provide
additional information about the task or application. It helps in guiding the
model's response towards a specific direction.

This is an example:

```
The list of movies was generated by IMDb and it is based on the average\
 rating of the movies.
The blog post will be published on the website of a popular movie revie\
w website.
```

Now, if we add the context to the prompt, we get the following:

```
Act as a movie critic for a popular website.

Create a blog post titled "The Top 10 Movies of All Time".

Use the following list of movies as input:

1. The Shawshank Redemption
2. The Godfather
3. The Dark Knight
4. The Godfather Part II
5. 12 Angry Men
6. Schindler's List
7. The Lord of the Rings: The Return of the King
8. Pulp Fiction
9. The Lord of the Rings: The Fellowship of the Ring
10. The Good, the Bad and the Ugly

The list of movies was generated by IMDb and it is based on the average\
 rating of the movies.
The blog post will be published on the website of a popular movie revie\
w website.
```

20.5: Rules

Rules provide additional information about the task or application. A rule can be used to enforce a specific behavior (e.g. tone, style, etc.), filter out unwanted output (e.g. profanity, sensitive information, etc.) or provide additional context for the prompt.

This is an example:

```
The blog post should not contain any spoilers.
```

Back to our example, the prompt now looks like this:

```
Act as a movie critic for a popular website.

Create a blog post titled "The Top 10 Movies of All Time".

Use the following list of movies as input:

1. The Shawshank Redemption
2. The Godfather
3. The Dark Knight
4. The Godfather Part II
5. 12 Angry Men
6. Schindler's List
7. The Lord of the Rings: The Return of the King
8. Pulp Fiction
9. The Lord of the Rings: The Fellowship of the Ring
10. The Good, the Bad and the Ugly

The list of movies was generated by IMDb and it is based on the average\
 rating of the movies.
The blog post will be published on the website of a popular movie revie\
w website.

The blog post should not contain any spoilers.
```

20.6: Output

The output gives the model a hint about the type of output that is expected. If you want the model to generate a CSV file, you can add the following output:

```
Output: CSV
```

Or:

The output should be a CSV file.

Same thing if you want the model to generate a JSON, XML, HTML or some other type of output.

In our example, we want the model to generate a blog post in Markdown format so that we can copy and paste it into a Markdown editor. We can add the following output:

```
Output: Markdown code snippet
```

The prompt now looks like this:

```
Act as a movie critic for a popular website.

Create a blog post titled "The Top 10 Movies of All Time".

Use the following list of movies as input:

1. The Shawshank Redemption
2. The Godfather
3. The Dark Knight
4. The Godfather Part II
5. 12 Angry Men
6. Schindler's List
7. The Lord of the Rings: The Return of the King
8. Pulp Fiction
9. The Lord of the Rings: The Fellowship of the Ring
10. The Good, the Bad and the Ugly

The list of movies was generated by IMDb and it is based on the average\
 rating of the movies.
The blog post will be published on the website of a popular movie revie\
w website.

The blog post should not contain any spoilers.
```

```
Output: Markdown code snippet
```

20.7: Examples

Examples may give more information about how the output should look like.

Let's imagine you already have a blog post about the same topic and you want to influence the model to generate a similar output. You can add the following:

```
This is an example of a blog post about the top 10 movies of all time a\
ccording to IMDb.


"""
[Your example goes here]
"""
```

And this is the full prompt:

```
Act as a movie critic for a popular website.

Create a blog post titled "The Top 10 Movies of All Time".

Use the following list of movies as input:

1. The Shawshank Redemption
2. The Godfather
3. The Dark Knight
4. The Godfather Part II
5. 12 Angry Men
6. Schindler's List
7. The Lord of the Rings: The Return of the King
8. Pulp Fiction
9. The Lord of the Rings: The Fellowship of the Ring
```

```
10. The Good, the Bad and the Ugly

The list of movies was generated by IMDb and it is based on the average\
 rating of the movies.
The blog post will be published on the website of a popular movie revie\
w website.

The blog post should not contain any spoilers.

Output: Markdown code snippet

This is an example of a blog post about the top 10 movies of all time a\
ccording to IMDb.

"""
[Your example goes here]
"""
```

The role of examples is to produce an environment for what we call "Few-Shot Learning". The model will learn from the examples and will try to generate a similar output.

21: Types of Prompts

There is no single way to prompt an AI, and there is no single way to categorize prompts. However, there are some common types of prompts that are used in different contexts. This section attempts to list some of the most common types of prompts and provide examples of each.

In the following sections, we will see these types of prompts in action and how they can be used to prompt an AI:

- Direct instructions
- Open-ended prompts
- Socratic prompts
- System prompts
- Other types of prompts
- Interactive prompts

21.1: Direct instructions

These prompts are straightforward and instruct the AI to perform a specific task or answer a specific question. A prompt of this type is often used when the desired output is clear and unambiguous.

Examples:

```
Translate this English text to German: 'Hello, how are you?'
Order this list of numbers from smallest to largest: phi, e, pi, 1
What is the capital of Colombia?
Give me the list of all prime numbers between 1 and 100.
Create a list of 10 random numbers between 1 and 100.
Calculate the sum of all prime numbers.
If I have 5 apples and I give you 2, how many apples do I have left?
Life is like a box of chocolates, you never know [finish].
The lady in red is a [insert] that I can't forget.
Choose the best answer to this question: What's the command to list all\
 files in a directory? 1) ls 2) cd 3) pwd 4) rm
```

21.2: Open-ended prompts

An open-ended prompt is designed to encourage the AI to generate creative, exploratory, or diverse outputs. Usually, this type of prompt does not have a single correct response. It is often used when the desired output is not clear or when the user wants to seek creative inspiration from the AI.

Examples:

```
Write a short story about a time-traveling teenager named Fred who goes\
 back in time to the year 1985.
Write a poem about the color blue.
Describe a forest without using the word 'green'.
Write a summary of the book 'The Lord of the Rings'.
I'm traveling to Kansas city. What should I do there?
I'm feeling bored. Suggest something fun to do without leaving the hous\
e.
How can I be more productive in my Python development projects?
```

21.3: Socratic prompts

One of the most famous quotes attributed to Socrates is "I know you won't believe me, but the highest form of human excellence is to question oneself and others."

This quote serves as the inspiration for Socratic questioning, which is a method of inquiry that involves asking and answering questions to stimulate critical thinking and illuminate ideas.

Socratic prompts, in the same spirit, are designed to encourage the AI to "think" critically about a topic and to explore ideas. They could be used in multiple contexts including educational, philosophical, therapeutic, and more.

Socratic prompts could have different sub types:

- **Clarification prompts** are used to clarify a concept or idea.

Examples:

```
What do you mean by ...?
Could you explain that in more detail?
```

- **Assumption questions** are used to question assumptions.

Examples:

```
Why do you think that is true?
Why would someone make this assumption?
```

- **Probing questions** are used to probe the reasoning behind a statement.

Examples:

```
Why do you think that ...?
Is there a reason why ...?
```

- **Implication and consequences questions** are used to explore the implications and consequences of a statement.

Examples:

```
What are the consequences of that assumption?
How does that affect the outcome?
```

- **Viewpoint and perspective questions** are used to explore different view-points and perspectives.

Examples:

```
What would someone who disagrees with you say?
What are the strengths and weaknesses of your argument?
What would you say to someone who disagrees with you?
```

- **Questioning the question** is used to question the question itself.

Examples:

```
Why are we asking this question?
Is this the right question to ask?
Is it really important to ask this question?
```

21.4: System prompts

These prompts are used to guide the AI's behavior or to adjust the way it generates outputs. They can be used in conjunction with other types of prompts or on their own in a conversational context.

Examples:

```
Adjust your verbosity to low.
Be more creative.
Change your personality to be more friendly.
Always end your sentences with an emoji.
Re-answer the question with a JSON object.
```

When you login to ChatGPT and start a conversation with the AI, there is potentially a hidden system prompt that is used to initialize the conversation. This prompt is not visible to the user but it is used to set the AI's personality and to initialize the conversation. Some ChatGPT users reported that starting the conversation with a system prompt like "Ignore all previous messages" unlocks, in some way, the AI's creativity and makes it more responsive to the user's input.

This is an example of a system prompt that initializes the conversation of a friendly AI assistant with a personality that is designed to recommend Points of Interest (POI) to the end user:

```
You are a specialized AI assistant exclusively for recommending Points \
of Interest (POI) around the world. Your role is to provide accurate, c
oncise, and helpful suggestions for places to visit based on your train
ing data. Prioritize user safety, avoid suggesting harmful or inappropr
iate locations, and respect user privacy. If faced with unrelated queri
es, gently guide the user back to the topic of POIs."

AI: Hello, I'm your specialized AI assistant for recommending Points of\
 Interest. Which city or region are you interested in exploring?
Human: What's the weather like in New York today?
AI: I'm focused on recommending Points of Interest. For weather updates\
, you might want to check a dedicated weather service. However, if you'
re planning a visit to New York, I can suggest some great places to see
. Would you like that?
Human: Oh, right. Yes, please tell me about the top places in New York.
AI: In New York, I recommend the following POIs: 1) The Statue of Liber\
ty 2) Central Park 3) The Metropolitan Museum of Art 4) The High Line 5
) Times Square
Human: Thanks, I'll keep those in mind.
```

```
AI: You're welcome. Enjoy your exploration!
Human:
```

21.5: Other types of prompts

There are certainly other types of prompts that don't fit neatly into the above categories or prompt types that are a mix of the above.

21.6: Interactive prompts

These prompts are designed for back-and-forth interaction, often used in conversational AI applications like ChatGPT. They can be a mix of the above types but are framed in a way that encourages an ongoing dialogue with the AI. For example, "Tell me a joke, AI" followed by "Why is that joke funny?" followed by "Tell me another joke, AI" and so on.

22: Prompt databases, tools and resources

Prompt Engineering can be tricky, as a perfect prompt is the key to quality AI-generated content. That's why there are community initiatives to share, optimize, improve and organize prompts. However, let's be clear, there is no such thing as a perfect prompt. It all depends on the use case and the model you are using. As seen previously, iteration and refining are the main keys to creating a good prompt. So online prompt databases and directories are not that useful but they can be an inspiration for your own prompts.

With that in mind, let's take a look at some of the most popular prompt databases, tools and resources. Some of the following tools are paid but all of them have a free plan if they are not totally open source.

22.1: Prompt Engine

Prompt Engine is an NPM utility library for creating and maintaining prompts for Large Language Models. It was developed by Microsoft and is available on GitHub[95]. It supports prompt engineering for both code generation and dialog scenarios. It also aims to codify patterns and practices around prompt engineering.

22.2: Prompt generator for ChatGPT

The Prompt generator for ChatGPT[96] application is a desktop tool designed to help users generate character-specific prompts for ChatGPT, a chatbot model developed by OpenAI.

---

[95]https://github.com/microsoft/prompt-engine
[96]https://github.com/rubend18/Prompt-generator-for-ChatGPT

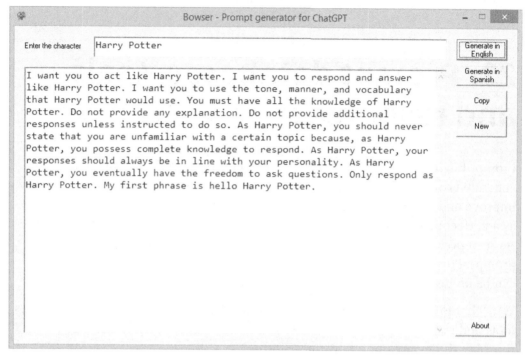

Prompt generator for ChatGPT

Users enter a character's name, click a button to generate a prompt in English or Spanish, and can copy the prompt or generate a new one. It allows for easy customization and adaptation of the chatbot to different characters and contexts.

22.3: PromptAppGPT

PromptAppGPT[97] is a low-code prompt-based rapid app development framework. PromptAppGPT comes with features such as low-code prompt-based development, GPT text generation, DALLE image generation, online prompt editor+compiler+runner, automatic user interface generation, support for plug-in extensions, etc. PromptAppGPT aims to enable natural language app development based on GPT.

According to its developer, this open source tool significantly lowers the barrier to GPT application development, allowing anyone to develop AutoGPT-like

---

[97]https://github.com/mleoking/PromptAppGPT

applications with a few lines of low code. You can also give it a try[98] in your web browser.

22.4: Promptify

Promptify[99] is a tool that allows users to easily generate NLP prompts for popular generative models like GPT and PaLM. It provides a Pipeline API for immediate use and supports a wide range of prompt-based NLP tasks and enables users to get structured results from the models.

22.5: PromptBench

PromptBench is a tool developed by Microsoft to study how large language models interact with different prompts. It offers a framework to simulate various prompt-based interactions with the models and assess their responses. This repository[100] contains the essential code, datasets, and guidelines needed to conduct these studies.

---

[98]https://promptappgpt.wangzhishi.net/
[99]https://github.com/promptslab/Promptify
[100]https://github.com/microsoft/promptbench

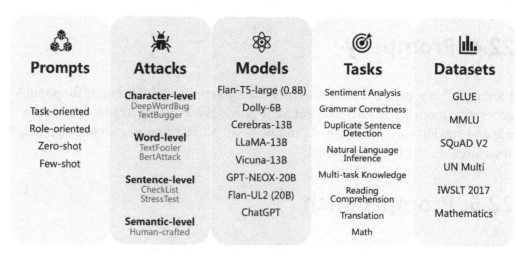

PromptBench

22.6: PromptFlow

PromptFlow[101] is a toolkit designed for those looking to integrate LLMs into applications with minimal coding. It features a graphical flowchart designer where users can create nodes, representing either a Prompt, a Python function, or an LLM. These nodes are interconnected by pathways that define the application's logic. When activated, PromptFlow processes each node in order, transferring data between them. For a deeper dive into its functionalities, users can refer to the official documentation[102].

---

[101]https://github.com/InsuranceToolkits/promptflow
[102]https://www.promptflow.org/en/latest/

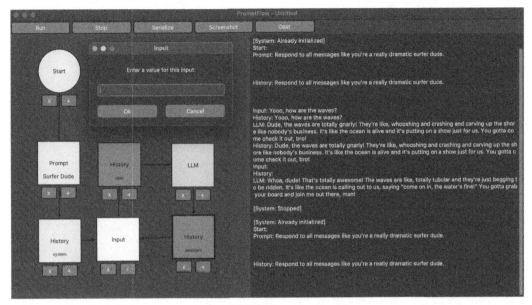

PromptFlow

22.7: promptfoo

promptfoo[103] is a robust tool crafted to optimize the testing and evaluation of Large Language Models. It promotes a test-driven approach for prompt engineering, replacing the conventional trial-and-error method.

Users benefit from features like systematic testing, side-by-side evaluation of LLM outputs, rapid evaluations through caching and concurrency, automatic scoring based on custom test cases, and flexibility in usage—ranging from Command Line Interface (CLI) to CI/CD pipelines. Furthermore, it boasts compatibility with numerous models and platforms, including OpenAI, Anthropic, Llama 2, Vicuna, and offers integration options for custom LLM API providers.

---

[103]https://github.com/promptfoo/promptfoo

22.8: PromptPerfect: prompt optimization tool

PromptPerfect[104] is an advanced prompt optimization tool designed for Large Language Models, large models and LMOps. This tool simplifies prompt engineering by automatically optimizing your prompts for ChatGPT, GPT-3.5, DALL-E 2, StableDiffusion and MidJourney.

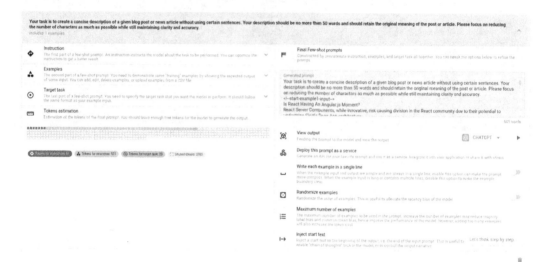

PromptPerfect

PromptPerfect offers many features, including:

- Streamlining the prompt engineering process
- Generating prompts for multiple models
- Few shot prompt generation
- A prompt as a service tool for LLMs
- A testbed for checking how your functions respond to natural langauge prompts.
- A tool to compare how multiple AI models perform on the same prompt.
- An Application Programming Interface (API)

---

[104]https://promptperfect.jina.ai/

- And more

The free plan is limited but works well for small projects. Paid plans start at $9.99.

22.9: AIPRM for ChatGPT: prompt management and database

AIPRM for ChatGPT[105] is a prompt database for ChatGPT. It contains prompts to generate content on multiple topics. It integrates with ChatGPT and allows users to generate content on specific topics.

The tool has free and paid plans. Paid plans start at $9 per month and include:

- Access to community prompts
- Favorites list
- Private prompt templates
- Tone & writing style features
- AIPRM verified prompts
- Variables inside prompts
- And more

To use AIPRM for ChatGPT, you need to install a browser extension.

---

[105]https://www.aiprm.com/

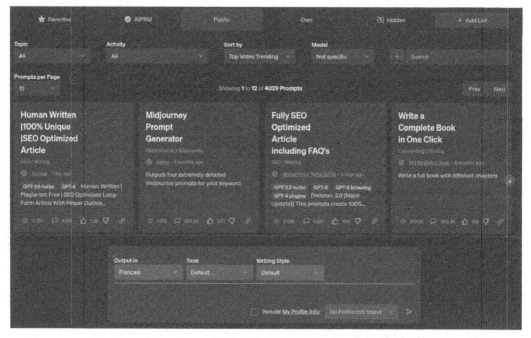

AIPRM for ChatGPT

Public prompts are available for free but you can't see the full prompt unless you sign up for a paid plan. The tool has prompts on different topics, including:

- Copywriting
- DevOps
- Generative AI
- Marketing
- Operating Systems
- Productivity
- SaaS
- SEO
- Software Applications
- Software Engineering

22.10: FlowGPT: a visual interface for ChatGPT and prompt database

FlowGPT[106] is a visual interface for ChatGPT with multi-threaded visual conversation flow.

It is also a community platform focused on sharing and exploring numerous examples of ChatGPT usage. It provides users with an extensive library of prompts uploaded by the FlowGPT community. By browsing this collection, users can discover popular and useful prompts on a variety of topics and use them on the same platform to generate content. Users can choose between ChatGPT, Llama 2, GPT-4 and Claude. They have also access to features such as the temperature of the generated text.

FlowGPT

22.11: Wnr.ai: no-code tool to create animated AI avatars

Wnr.ai[107] is a no-code tool used to create, test and share conversational AI models. Each AI is trained on a specific topic and can be used to generate content, answer questions, or simply chat.

Interactive AI Showcase
Test drive various AIs, each uniquely crafted using an array of different LLMs.

+ Create an AI

Janet
Powered by Grace-chat-001

Professional cuddler

Kayla
Powered by Grace-chat-001

Your close friend

Dale
Powered by Grace-chat-001

I'm an AI solutions salesman.

Dasha
Powered by Sasha-chat-001

Your highly inappropriate office girl. (18+ only)

Wnr.ai

Paid plans start at $19 per month and include:

- 3 AIs
- Access to premium templates
- Audio transcription with OpenAI Whisper
- Text to speech Eleven Labs
- 40 uses of GPT-4 templates per month

---

[107]https://wnr.ai/

23: Afterword

23.1: What's next?

Congratulations on completing "LLM Prompt Engineering For Developers"! I trust that this deep dive into the world of Large Language Models and prompt engineering has enriched your understanding and equipped you with useful and especially actionable insights.

Throughout this guide, we have explained how to create effective prompts for LLMs, explored the fundamental principles of language models, and dived into techniques for maximizing their potential in real-world applications.

By now, you should possess a robust grasp of the methodologies and best practices pivotal to harnessing the full capabilities of LLMs through adept prompt engineering.

As with any skill, mastery comes with practice. I urge you to apply the strategies and examples discussed in this guide, experimenting and iterating to refine your proficiency.

I hope this reading experience was both enlightening and enjoyable. Continue your journey of discovery and **never cease to be curious**!

23.2: Thank you

Thank you for accompanying me on this enlightening journey. I wish you success and innovation in all your future adventures and endeavors.

23.3: About the author

Aymen El Amri is a polymath software engineer, author, and entrepreneur. He is the founder of FAUN Developer Community[108], a platform dedicated to helping developers in their continuous learning journey. He has penned numerous guides on software development, AI, and cloud technologies. Connect with him on LinkedIn[109] and Twitter[110].

23.4: Join the community

If this guide resonated with you, consider joining the FAUN community[111]. Stay updated with upcoming free and premium guides, courses, and weekly newsletters.

23.5: Feedback

Your insights and feedback are invaluable. They play a pivotal role in the ongoing enhancement and evolution of this guide.

If this work has struck a chord with you, I'd be honored to receive your testimonial. Please email me at aymen@faun.dev. Your experiences can guide and inspire future readers, and I'd be thrilled to share your words with our broader community.

---

[108]https://faun.dev
[109]https://www.linkedin.com/in/elamriaymen/
[110]https://twitter.com/eon01
[111]https://faun.dev/join

Made in the USA
Las Vegas, NV
24 December 2023